# Turtle

2nd Edition

## Lenny Flank Jr.

BICENTENNIAL
1807
WILEY
2007
BICENTENNIAL

Wiley Publishing, Inc.

Copyright © 2007 by Wiley Publishing, Inc., Hoboken, New Jersey. All rights reserved.

Howell Book House
Published by Wiley Publishing, Inc., Hoboken, New Jersey

***Library of Congress Cataloging-in-Publication Data:***
Flank, Lenny.
  Turtle : your happy healthy pet / Lenny Flank Jr. — 2nd ed.
    p. cm.
  Includes bibliographical references and index.
    ISBN 978-0-470-03791-1 (cloth : alk. paper)
  1. Turtles as pets. I. Title.
  SF459.T8F53 2007
  639.3'92—dc22

Book design by Melissa Auciello-Brogan
Cover design by Michael J. Freeland
Wiley Bicentennial Logo: Richard J. Pacifico
Book production by Wiley Publishing, Inc. Composition Services

# About the Author

**Lenny Flank Jr.** is a longtime reptile keeper and enthusiast who has kept more than 100 different species over the past 25 years. He has written five books about reptiles, amphibians, and invertebrates, and has also written articles for *Reptiles* magazine and *Reptile and Amphibian Hobbyist* magazine.

For several years, Lenny did reptile rescue work, taking in unwanted snakes, turtles, and lizards, providing them with needed rehabilitation, and then adopting them out to good homes. As part of his education and public outreach efforts, he has given numerous educational talks and shows, using live reptiles, for school classrooms, Scout troops, and environmental groups.

Lenny lives in St Petersburg, Florida, where he shares his apartment with four snakes, two tarantulas, and a 10-year-old Musk turtle named Muffin.

# About Howell Book House

Since 1961, Howell Book House has been America's premier publisher of pet books. We're dedicated to companion animals and the people who love them, and our books reflect that commitment. Our stable of authors—training experts, veterinarians, breeders, and other authorities—is second to none. And we've won more Maxwell Awards from the Dog Writers Association of America than any other publisher.

As we head toward the half-century mark, we're more committed than ever to providing new and innovative books, along with the classics our readers have grown to love. This year, we're launching several exciting new initiatives, including redesigning the Howell Book House logo and revamping our biggest pet series, Your Happy Healthy Pet™, with bold new covers and updated content. From bringing home a new puppy to competing in advanced equestrian events, Howell has the titles that keep animal lovers coming back again and again.

# Contents

# Shopping List

You'll need to do a bit of stocking up before you bring your turtle home. Below is a basic list of must-have supplies. For more detailed information on the selection of each item below, consult chapter 5. For specific guidance on what food you'll need, review chapter 6.

### For aquatic turtles:

- ☐ Tank
- ☐ Tank stand
- ☐ Heat lamp for basking
- ☐ Water heater
- ☐ Thermometer
- ☐ UV fluorescent light
- ☐ External water filter
- ☐ Rocks, log, or wood for basking
- ☐ 5-gallon bucket
- ☐ Siphon hose

### For terrestrial turtles:

- ☐ Tank
- ☐ Tank stand
- ☐ Heat lamp for basking
- ☐ Thermometer
- ☐ UV fluorescent light
- ☐ Substrate
- ☐ Hide box
- ☐ Water pan
- ☐ Food dish

There are likely to be a few other items that you're dying to pick up before bringing your turtle home. Use the following blanks to note any additional items you'll be shopping for.

- ☐ _____
- ☐ _____
- ☐ _____
- ☐ _____
- ☐ _____
- ☐ _____
- ☐ _____
- ☐ _____

# Pet Sitter's Guide

We can be reached at (\_\_)\_\_\_\_\_-_____ Cellphone (\_\_)\_\_\_\_\_-_____

We will return on _____ (date) at _____ (approximate time)

Other individual to contact in case of emergency _____

_____

Turtle species: _____

## Care Instructions

In the following blank lines, let the sitter know what to feed, how much, and when; what tasks need to be performed daily; and what weekly tasks they'll be responsible for.

Morning_____

_____

_____

_____

_____

_____

Evening _____

_____

_____

_____

_____

Other tasks and special instructions _____

_____

_____

_____

_____

_____

# Part I
# All About Turtles

# The Turtle

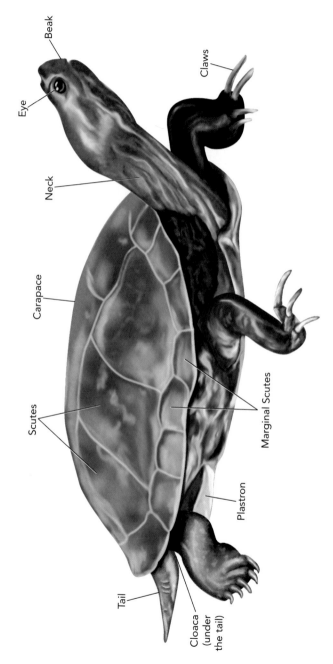

Beak

Eye

Neck

Claws

Carapace

Scutes

Marginal Scutes

Plastron

Tail

Cloaca (under the tail)

# Chapter 1

# What Is a Turtle?

There is perhaps no more easily recognizable animal on earth than a turtle. Although there are lizards who look like snakes and salamanders who look like lizards, no other living creature looks remotely like a turtle. With their calm dispositions and brightly colored shells, turtles have been spared the enmity with which most other reptiles are usually regarded. Unlike lizards and snakes, which are almost universally reviled, turtles are usually considered charming and attractive creatures. Few people, even the most intense reptile haters, are afraid of turtles.

A few decades ago, every convenience store in the country was stocked with tiny, bright green baby turtles, usually found in a shallow water tray complete with a tiny plastic island and a palm tree. Unfortunately, few of the many thousands of people who purchased these little creatures had any real idea how to care for them, and most of them ended up in a watery grave after a few months. This dreadful mortality rate, combined with some exaggerated fears about the spread of disease by turtles, virtually put an end to the turtle pet trade.

Today, however, we have become more knowledgeable about the natural world and the role that various animals play in it—including reptiles—and turtles have once again become popular pets.

This book was written as a guide for the beginning turtle keeper, so new hobbyists can keep their pets happy and healthy. Although keeping turtles and tortoises in captivity is not difficult, there are a few potential problems that turtle keepers must be aware of, and a few rules and procedures that must be followed if these animals are to thrive in captivity.

Our knowledge of how to meet the needs of captive reptiles has expanded enormously in the past few years, and even though this book is aimed primarily at beginners, I hope that it can serve as a useful reference for more experienced turtle keepers, as well.

# The Biology of Turtles and Tortoises

There are about 220 species of turtles living today—less than one-tenth th
number of living snakes or lizards. Despite their relative lack of diversity, how
ever, turtles are hardy and adaptable animals, and have moved into a wide vari
ety of habitats, from hot, arid deserts to the open seas.

In size, they range from the tiny Musk turtle, less than 5 inches long, to th
huge marine Leatherback, which reaches lengths of over 6 feet and weighs mor
than half a ton. The largest living land turtle, the Galapagos tortoise, can reac
a length of 4½ feet and weigh more than 550 pounds.

All turtles are reptiles, a class of animals characterized by dry scaly skin, a
dependence upon external heat sources rather than internal metabolism, and a
shelled egg that can be laid on land.

## Ectothermic Animals

Like all other reptiles and amphibians, turtles are ectothermic, meaning they can
not produce their own internal body heat. Such a system of metabolism is some
times called "cold-blooded," but this is not a very accurate term, since some deser
tortoises maintain a body temperature of more than 100 degrees Fahrenheit.

The word *ectothermic* comes from the Latin words for "outside heat," and this
is a better description of how the turtle's metabolism functions. In all animals

*Ectotherms like the turtle cannot produce enough body heat to maintain their temperature at a specific
level, so they must get their heat from their environment. Hot desert areas therefore have a wide variety
of turtles.*

## Turtle Terminology

Turtles make up the order of reptiles known as Chelonia, which is further divided into two groups: the Cryptodirans (characterized by the ability to pull their heads into their shells by folding their neck vertically) and the Pleurodirans (or side-necked turtles, who retract their heads under the margin of their shells by folding their necks sideways). The vast majority of living turtles belong to the Cryptodiran group.

I have often been asked what the difference is between a turtle, a terrapin, and a tortoise. The word *turtle,* as it's used in everyday language, refers to any member of the Chelonian order—any reptile with a shell. The word *tortoise* is usually used to refer to those Chelonians who live primarily on land and rarely enter water. *Terrapin* usually applies to those turtles who live along streams or ponds and are largely aquatic.

These names have no scientific standing, however; they are simply common names used by nonspecialists. To a biologist, there are no technical distinctions between turtles and terrapins, although usually the term *tortoise* is reserved solely for the members of the Testudidine group of land turtles, and the word *terrapin* most often refers specifically to the Diamondback terrapin of the eastern United States. All the shelled reptiles are members of the order Chelonia, and all Chelonians can correctly be referred to as turtles.

including reptiles, biological processes are controlled by a class of chemicals known as enzymes, and these enzymes work best at rather high temperatures. In "warm-blooded" animals, such as mammals, the heat that is released during metabolism is used to warm the body and maintain the proper temperature for these enzymes, no matter what the environmental temperature might be. A human being, for instance, maintains a body temperature of close to 98.6 degrees Fahrenheit, whether the air temperature is 100 degrees or 50 degrees.

Ectotherms, however, cannot produce enough body heat from their own metabolism to maintain their body temperature at a specific level. Therefore they would take on the same body temperature as their surroundings. To prevent this, and to maintain a suitable body temperature, reptiles must use external sources of heat to keep their internal temperature high enough. That is why turtles are most often seen basking on logs or rocks in the sun; they are using the heat provided by the sun to raise their body temperature to an acceptable level.

This need to maintain and conserve body heat is one of the most important factors in any turtle's life. In hot environments, such as Latin American and African deserts, it is easy for the turtle to maintain a high body temperature; therefore, semiarid and desert areas have a wide variety of turtles.

Because water can retain heat more effectively than air, aquatic habitats in warm areas also provide the all-important external heat needed by turtles. The largest living turtles are entirely aquatic, and live either in warm, shallow rivers and lakes or in the open seas. Here the ambient temperature is so high that the turtle can afford to develop a large, heavy body—something that would take an unacceptably long time to heat up in cooler areas.

In fact, the large sea turtles, such as Leatherbacks, have such large bodies that they can retain more body heat (which is continuously produced by the action of their swimming muscles) than they lose through their body surface. This enables them to maintain body temperatures that are several degrees higher than the surrounding ocean water.

In cooler, temperate regions, such as North America and Europe, it is more difficult for turtles to stay warm. As a result, turtles from cooler areas are typically smaller and darker in color than tropical turtles (so they can absorb sunlight and heat themselves up faster). In the winter, when short days and colder temperatures make it impossible to maintain the best body temperature, turtles will bury themselves deep in the mud, below the frost line, and hibernate, slowing down virtually all of their body functions. These turtles emerge in the spring when the days grow longer and the temperatures get warmer.

# Chelonian Anatomy

The most obvious characteristic of turtles is, of course, the shell. It varies from the leathery carapace of the Softshell turtle, which contains hardly any bone at all, to the thick casing of the Box turtle, which can make up to one-third of the animal's total body weight. The shell is made from bony plates in the skin that have fused to the rib cage. The internal anatomy of the turtle, particularly the breathing apparatus and the pelvis and shoulder bones (also called the limb girdles), have been heavily modified to accommodate the shell.

## The Eyes

Turtles have excellent vision and can detect motion at a considerable distance. They can also detect the outlines of potential predators, even if the intruder is not moving. Along with their keen sense of smell, turtles use their eyesight as the primary way of finding food. According to most scientists, turtles are able to see in color, and are particularly sensitive to reds and yellows (they can also sense a range of infrared wavelengths that are invisible to humans).

*Many turtles are predators, and their keen eyesight helps them locate and catch their prey.*

Turtle eyes have two large tear ducts (called lachrymal glands), and in some turtles—particularly the marine turtles, who ingest large quantities of salt water with their food—these lachrymal glands are used to excrete excess salt from the body in the form of thick, gel-like "tears."

## The Skull

The turtle skull is heavy and solid, with very thick bones. Turtles lack the holes between skull bones that other reptiles possess. In all the other reptiles—snakes, lizards, and crocodilians—the skull has two distinct holes, called *fossae*, through which the jaw muscles are attached from the temporal area of the skull, just behind the eyes, to the rear portion of the jawbones. Turtles don't have these fossae, and their jaw muscles run along the outside of the skull without passing through any holes, which enables these muscles to expand outward when the jaws are closed.

All turtles lack teeth, and instead have a sharp-edged, horny jaw sheath. Since they cannot chew, turtles must eat by tearing off bite-sized chunks of food using their front claws and their powerful jaws. Predatory turtles, such as Snappers and Big Headed turtles, have sharp, hooklike projections at the tips of their jaws, shaped somewhat like an eagle's beak, to help them hold and tear at prey. Plant eaters have toothlike, serrated jaw margins that enable them to cut and bite through tough plant stems.

## The Tongue

Turtles, like snakes and lizards and many types of mammals, have a structure in the roof of their mouth called the Jacobson's organ, which is used to detect airborne chemicals. Even though they cannot extend their tongues the way snakes and lizards can, turtles are able to use their thick, fleshy tongues to capture scent particles in the air and transfer these to the Jacobson's organ. The Jacobson's organ is directly connected to the brain by the olfactory nerve. Turtles, thus, have a keen sense of smell, even underwater. To smell underwater, the turtle will open his mouth slightly, drawing in a small amount of water through the nostrils and passing this through the Jacobson's organ before expelling it from the mouth.

In many turtles, the tongue is thick and immovable, and cannot be used for swallowing in the normal manner. These turtles can only swallow underwater, where they can use the rush of water to push food down their throats.

## The Lungs

Because the shell prevents the chest from expanding, turtles must use a special set of muscles in the body to expand and contract the size of their chest cavity by moving some of the internal organs around, pumping air in and out of the lungs like a bellows. The hiss that you often hear when picking up a turtle is not intended as a threat, but is simply the sound made by air being rapidly pushed out of the lungs to make room for the head as it is pulled under the shell.

*Special adaptations in the throat and cloaca enable some turtles to extract oxygen from either air or water, so they can stay under water for long periods.*

In addition, many turtles use a method of breathing called gular pumping, in which the throat is expanded to draw in air, which is then pushed down into the lungs. This throat action is made possible by the large, moveable hyoid bone located in the neck. Some turtles are also capable of using the lining of the throat and cloaca, the cavity into which the digestive, urinary, and reproductive tracts empty, to extract oxygen from either air or water. During hibernation, turtles depend completely upon gular pumping and cloacal breathing for all of their reduced oxygen needs.

## The Heart

Like all reptiles (with the exception of the crocodiles), turtles have a three-chambered heart consisting of two upper chambers and one lower chamber, incompletely divided by a muscular wall. The blood is pumped to the lungs by one of the two upper chambers, known as atria, and returns to the single lower chamber, called the ventricle. Here it mixes with the oxygen-depleted blood returning from the rest of the body. This mixture of oxygen-rich and oxygen-depleted blood is then pumped into the other atrium, where it enters the aortic arches and is distributed throughout the body.

This arrangement mixes unoxygenated blood returning from the body with the oxygenated blood returning from the lungs before it is passed on to the rest of the body. It is an inefficient method of distributing oxygen, and as a result, turtles tire easily and cannot sustain their activity for long periods of time without frequent stops to rest.

## The Shell

The turtle's shell is made up of a top part, called the carapace, and a bottom part, called the plastron. These are connected along the sides of the turtle to form the shell compartment. Both these shell parts are covered with horny plates, called scutes.

### The Scutes

The scutes are made of the protein keratin—the same substance that makes up human fingernails and hair. Scutes are made up of living tissue and contain nerve endings (a turtle can feel it when something is touching his shell). They do not have a large number of pain receptors, but if they are injured or damaged, they have remarkable regenerative powers. The rings that are visible on the scutes of some turtles represent alternate periods of growth and nongrowth, and can sometimes be used to roughly estimate the age of the turtle.

The multiple scutes overlap the underlying bony plates; this strengthens the shell. The scutes are also decorated with colors and patterns that are specific to each species. If a turtle happens to be missing a scute, the bony seams of the carapace are often visible. Damaged scutes are vulnerable to fungal infections.

> **CAUTION**
>
> The once common practice of painting the shells of turtles can kill the scutes and infect the underlying bone, causing severe injury.

Commercial tortoiseshell, which was once used in large amounts for combs and decorations, is actually the intricately patterned scutes of sea turtles, usually Green turtles or Loggerheads. The nearly insatiable demand for tortoiseshell led to widespread hunting of these turtles and their near extinction. Today, plastics made to look like tortoiseshell have replaced the real thing in most cases.

## The Carapace

The bony plates that make up the turtle's carapace develop from small, flat bones (sometimes called platelets) in the skin called ossicles or osteoderms, which have become fused to the turtle's rib cage and backbone. The shell is therefore permanently attached to the turtle's skeleton, and a living turtle cannot be removed from his shell.

*The arched design of carapace makes it very strong, and turtles are able to support a lot of weight on their shell. You can clearly see the scutes on these turtles.*

Because of their thickness and their vaulted construction (like the arched roof of a medieval church), turtle carapaces are incredibly strong. A full-grown Galapagos tortoise can easily support the weight of two or three adult humans on his shell. Despite its great strength, however, the carapace is vulnerable to sudden impacts, and can be severely cracked and damaged by a dropped object or a fall.

The Pancake tortoise of Africa is unique among the land tortoises in having large, open spaces in his carapace. These openings, called fontanelles, make the shell flexible, enabling the turtle to escape from predators by retreating deep into a crevice or crack and inflating his lungs to expand the shell and wedge himself tightly in a protective position.

The carapaces of terrestrial tortoises are high and dome-shaped. Since most terrestrial turtles eat plant matter, they must have large stomachs and long intestines to process such low-quality food. Aquatic turtles tend to be more carnivorous and can get by with smaller internal organs. Their shells tend to have a low, flat streamlined shape, which helps reduce drag as the turtle swims about.

## The Plastron

The plastron is the bottom portion of the turtle's shell. It is made up of four pairs of bony plates covered with keratin scutes. The plastron scutes, like those of the carapace, do not coincide with the bones of the plastron.

The plastron is not dragged on the ground when the turtle is walking, but is lifted clear by his legs. Still, the plastron scutes do wear off, and they are constantly being replaced. If the plastron is damaged (by being dragged over a sharp, rocky surface, for instance) the resulting wounds are easily invaded by fungus and can cause serious problems for the turtle.

In some species of turtles, such as Box turtles and Musk turtles, one

*If a turtle's plastron is damaged, serious infections can result.*

or two flexible hinges run across the plastron. This enables the turtle to fold his bottom shell and enclose himself tightly within.

## Skin Color

The green skin color found in many aquatic turtles is actually the result of the combination of two separate pigments, yellow and blue, in the lower layers of the skin. Some turtles are born lacking the blue pigment and thus appear yellowish rather than green; these turtles are said to be *leucistic*. An even rarer mutation can cause an absence of the yellow pigment, producing a bright blue turtle.

Occasionally, albino turtles—those with no skin pigment—are born. The Softshell turtles seem especially prone to albinism.

Some turtles have gaps or openings in the bony plates of the plastron and carapace, called fontanelles, which help make the shell lighter. These fontanelles are particularly large in the marine turtles, which must reduce the weight of their bodies to swim efficiently.

## The Limb Girdles

The reptilian pelvis is very different from that of mammals. In mammals, the limbs are underneath the body and the upper bones of the limbs descend in a straight line from the shoulder or hip joints. This enables mammals to carry their body weight efficiently atop their relatively straight legs. In reptiles, however, the joints in the pelvic and shoulder girdles face outward rather than down, forcing the upper limb bones to project out sideways instead of downward. This means that the reptile's feet are located far out to the sides of his body, rather than directly underneath it, as in mammals. Reptiles thus have a characteristic walking pose, with their legs bent out at the elbows and knees, which makes them look as if they are halfway through a push-up.

Although they have the sprawling gait typical of all reptiles, turtles have limb structures that are even more unusual among vertebrates. In most vertebrates, the shoulder and pelvic girdles are on the outside of the rib cage. Because of their shell, turtles have their limb girdles inside their rib cage. The basic effect is that leg mobility is severely limited—hence the proverbially slow turtle.

Despite their reputation for slowness, turtles have strong legs and some species are capable of moving quickly over land for short distances. A number of turtles, particularly those with long legs or smaller plastrons (including Wood and Musk turtles), are excellent climbers, and can easily scale trees or even chain-link fences.

Most turtles are pigeon-toed, and walk with their feet turned inward. In the aquatic turtles, the toes are webbed and the claws are long and sharp. Terrestrial tortoises have short, blunt toes and a somewhat flattened, elephantlike foot designed for digging and burrowing.

## The Cloaca

The cloaca is the single opening under the tail for the turtle's digestive, urinary, and reproductive tracts. Aquatic turtles excrete most of their waste in the form of water-soluble urea, as do mammals. Terrestrial tortoises, who need to conserve their use of water, excrete their waste in the form of dry crystals of uric acid, as do snakes and lizards.

> ### Did You Know?
> The Box turtle can seal himself so tightly that a knife blade cannot even be inserted into the shell. These turtles are capable of staying closed up for an hour or more, without breathing, until they sense danger has passed.

# Turtle Reproduction

Turtles practice internal fertilization, in which the sperm is introduced directly into the female's cloaca by the male. Turtles have a single penis (male snakes and lizards have a pair of reproductive organs, called hemipenes) with a deep groove running down the middle through which the sperm flows. Female turtles are capable of storing live sperm for up to three years, and can lay viable eggs for several years after a single mating.

Turtle egg shells are formed inside the female by a series of excretions produced by the walls of the oviduct as the developing eggs move down the reproductive tract toward the cloaca. In some species, the eggs are soft and leathery; in most, however, they are hard like bird eggs. The shells of Snapping turtle eggs are so thick that they will often bounce if dropped.

The gestation period varies according to species but is usually between three to four months.

*Turtle mothers do not guard their eggs the way birds do, but they do take care to lay them in spots that are protected from predators.*

Turtle mothers are generally good at securing their eggs. Although no turtle incubates the eggs or guards the young after hatching, most turtles do take particular care in laying them in areas that are environmentally suitable and safe from predators. One exception is the Musk turtle, who has a habit of dropping her eggs right in the open—which is surprising since they lay very few eggs at a time. Apparently, predators don't like Musk turtle eggs very much.

## Chapter 2

# Turtle History

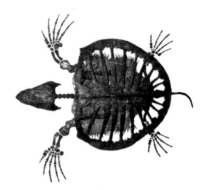

urtles, like all other living animals, are the products of the process of evolution, in which organisms change over time in response to changes in environmental conditions. Over a very long time, they change so much that they become different animals and thus form a new species.

Because of their thick, bony shells and their compact, heavy skulls, turtle remains can survive exposure to the elements much better than those of other animals, and thus become fossilized much more frequently. Turtle fossils are found more often than those of other animals of similar size, and the evolutionary history of the modern turtle is fairly well known. The earliest turtle ancestors, however, had no shells, and the exact ancestry of living turtles is disputed among paleontologists.

## Reptile Evolution

All reptiles are believed to have evolved from the large group of ancient amphibians known as Labrynthodonts. The evolutionary advance that set the reptiles apart from the amphibians was the development of the amniote egg. Animals have been laying eggs for millions of years, but they had to be laid in the water to keep the contents from drying out. The eggs of animals such as amphibians and fish still do.

However, the eggs of amniotes, a group that includes turtles, lizards, birds, dinosaurs, and some mammals, have a water-tight shell and a series of fluid-filled membranes that nourish and nurture the young inside. Amniote eggs can be laid on land, freeing the animal from the necessity of returning to the water for reproduction. The oldest known shelled egg was found in Texas and dates to the lower Permian period, more than 275 million years ago.

The earliest animal that can definitely be recognized as a reptile is a small creature known as *Hylonomus,* found in fossilized tree stumps in Nova Scotia dating back to the Carboniferous period, about 360 to 290 million years ago. *Hylonomus* was part of the group of reptiles known as Cotylosaurs, or "stem reptiles," which are believed to be the ancestors of all of the reptile families alive today.

# The Turtle's Early Ancestors

We do not know which group of stem reptiles gave rise to the turtles, but over the years several possibilities have been put forward. One early candidate for a turtle ancestor was *Eunotosaurus,* who had wide, paddle-shaped ribs that some considered as a primitive version of the modern turtle shell. Today, however, we know that turtle shells are not made from the ribs, but from bony plates in the skin. *Eunotosaurus* is no longer considered a possible turtle ancestor.

Because turtle skulls are solid and lack the holes, or fossae, found in other reptile skulls, it was long assumed that the turtles came directly from very primitive ancestors with similar skull features, known as anapsids. (Diapsids, by contrast, have two distinct holes in the skull through which the jaw muscles are attached.) Many authorities considered a group of stem reptiles known as Pareiasaurs as the true ancestors of turtles. These were large, heavy-bodied reptiles who lived in the early Triassic period (about 248 to 206 million years ago), just as the dinosaurs were rising to prominence. Many of the Pareiasaurs were armored with a layer of bony osteoderms embedded in the skin, somewhat like the bony plates on an alligator's back. And they had heavy, solid skulls, much like those of modern turtles. In addition to the Pareiasaurs, three or four other groups of primitive anapsid reptiles were also proposed at various times as possible turtle ancestors.

In recent years, however, the science of DNA sequencing has completely changed our view of early turtle evolution. By comparing the DNA of various living organisms,

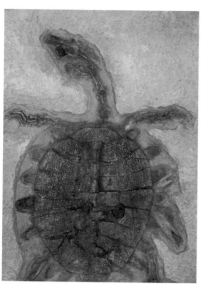
*This fossilized Softshell turtle was found in Wyoming. It is about 45 million years old and is a member of the Trionyx species.*

biologists can now determine which of them are most closely related to each other. And when the DNA of living reptiles was compared, it produced a surprise: Turtles are not primitive anapsids, as was previously thought. Instead, they are descendents of later diapsids, just like all the other reptiles, and the fossae in their skulls became filled in by bone as they evolved. DNA tests show that turtles are more closely related to the crocodiles than to any other reptile group. This means that none of the primitive anapsids can be turtle ancestors, and we must search instead among the early diapsids for a common ancestor between turtles and crocodilians.

We still have not, however, found any fossils from these earliest turtle ancestors. The earliest recognizable turtle, called *Proganochelys,* comes from about 225 million years ago, and already appeared somewhat similar to modern Snapping turtles (although, unlike the Snapper, these Triassic turtles lived on land).

> **Did You Know?**
>
> The scientific study of reptiles and amphibians is called *herpetology,* and reptiles and amphibians are usually referred to by experts as "herpetofauna" or "herptiles," which is usually shortened in conversation to "herps."

In the Jurassic period (about 206 to 144 million years ago), at the same time that dinosaurs were the dominant form of life on Earth, turtles were rapidly diversifying. Sea turtles from this period included *Plesiochelys,* who lived in Europe, and the Giant Sea turtle *Archelon,* who, at a length of 12 feet, is the largest turtle who ever lived.

All of these ancient turtles had several features unique to them that do not appear in any modern turtles. These features include a series of bony projections from the cervical vertebrae in the neck (which made it impossible for these turtles to withdraw their heads into their shells) and a larger number of vertebrae than any modern turtle has. It is possible that all of the ancient turtles discovered so far are side branches of turtle evolution that went extinct without descendants, and the real ancestors of modern turtles have yet to be found.

## The Appearance of Modern Turtles

The line that produced the turtle species we know today appears to have divided early in its history, into two separate groups, based on a different arrangement of the vertebrae in the neck. One group, the Cryptodirans, or hidden-necked, developed the ability to pull their heads straight back into their shells, bending their

*This New Guinea Snakeneck turtle is an example of a Pleurodiran. She pulls her long neck alongside her body for protection.*

neck into a vertical S-shaped curve. The other group, known as Pleurodirans, or side-necked, was able to pull their long necks alongside their bodies, underneath the margin of their shells.

The vast majority of turtles living today are Cryptodirans. Pleurodirans are a minority on most continents (they do not appear in North America at all).

The Mud and Musk families of turtles, which are closely related to Snappers and are the most primitive of the living turtles, appear to have evolved in North America shortly after dinosaurs went extinct at the end of the Cretaceous period, some 65 million years ago. The most ancient fossils of a still-living turtle species are those of Snapping turtles (*Chelydra serpentina*), which roamed over Europe, Asia, and North America more than 15 million years ago.

The Testudo group of modern land tortoises first appeared in Africa, and reached its greatest diversity in the dry, arid areas of the sub-Sahara. The varied Softshell family evolved in eastern Asia but is now found throughout the world.

The Emydid family, which includes Painted turtles, Sliders, and River Cooters, is the largest and most diverse of the modern turtles, and seems to be just beginning its evolutionary diversification. The most recent of the turtle groups to evolve seems to be the North American Box turtles. These appear to have given up their aquatic lifestyle for a terrestrial one very recently in geological time.

# Chelonian Ecology

In most ecosystems, the largest number of living organisms is plants, which use photosynthesis to manufacture their own food from sunlight and materials in their environment. Ecologists thus refer to plants as *producers*. Because animals cannot photosynthesize or manufacture their own food, their way to get food is to eat plants or other animals. This sequence, in which plants make food from sunlight, herbivores then eat the plants, the herbivores are eaten by carnivores who, in turn, are preyed upon by larger carnivores, is called the food chain.

Turtles, like all reptiles and amphibians, play a very important role in a number of different ecosystems, both as predator and as prey. In some habitats, such as deserts and shallow riverbanks, turtles are the most abundant mid-level predators—those in the middle of the food chain.

As predators, turtles help keep the populations of smaller prey animals, such as fish and frogs, in check. And as prey, turtles help support the populations of larger predators, such as alligators, crocodiles, jaguars, and others.

*Turtles occupy an important niche in all the ecosystems they inhabit. They help maintain the delicate balance among species.*

# Chapter 3

## The Best (and Worst) Turtles for Beginners

**W**hich turtle is the right one for you? To decide that, you'll have to start by asking yourself a few questions. What color and size turtle do you prefer? How much space can you dedicate to keeping the turtle? What sort of climatic conditions does the turtle need, and what can you provide? How often do you intend to interact with the turtle? Will your new turtle get along with any turtles you may already own?

Another very basic choice is whether you want a terrestrial species (who rarely enters the water) or an aquatic species (who spends most of his time in or at the edge of the water). In general, terrestrial turtles are easier to house and to care for, but also tend to be more expensive and a bit less tolerant of changes in environmental conditions.

If you intend to interact with your turtles, then you can probably rule out the aquatic species—they do not tolerate handling well, and are largely for watching rather than touching. The terrestrial tortoises, on the other hand, are usually responsive to their keepers.

Keep in mind, also, that turtles can get quite large, and live for a long time. That cute little Red-Eared Slider in the pet store will, in just a few years, be as big as a dinner plate, and can easily live twenty to thirty years. Financial considerations must be kept in mind as well. While some turtles, such as Painted turtles and Red-Eared Sliders, are very inexpensive, others who make excellent pets, such as Matamatas and Redfoot tortoises, can be quite expensive.

# The Best Turtles for Beginners

In general, a suitable turtle for a beginning herper should:

- Be docile and tame, and easy to handle
- Be medium in size as an adult
- Have a diet that is easy to provide
- Be able to tolerate a wide range of environmental conditions

Here, then, is my personal list of the best species for beginning hobbyists. Keep in mind that all turtle species have their own individual requirements, and, since a book such as this can one only provide general care information, every turtle keeper needs to obtain as much information as possible about each individual species before obtaining one.

## Aquatic Turtles

### Red-Eared Slider (*Trachemys elegans*)

This is probably the most widely kept reptile on earth, and is readily available captive-bred. Nearly every pet store that sells reptiles is likely to have a tank full of Red-Eared Sliders.

The Red-Eared Slider is an aquatic turtle and is native to the southeastern United States. As a youngster, he is bright green with red and yellow markings. With age, the color fades to a dark olive. Adults measure about 9 inches long.

These turtles like to bask and will need a fair-sized basking area. They are omnivores.

*Red-Eared Sliders are easy to find and easy to keep.*

### Painted Turtle (*Chrysemys picta*)

The Painted turtle is not as colorful as the young Red-Eared Slider but is still attractively marked with red-and-yellow stripes on an olive background.

There are four subspecies of the Painted turtle found throughout North America but all have similar needs and can be cared for the same way. Although not quite as abundant as the Red-Eared Slider, Painted turtles are widely bred and are inexpensive.

*The Painted turtle has a beautiful shell.*

*Florida Red-Bellied turtles make good tankmates for similar species.*

Adults grow to about 10 inches long. These turtles will require a basking area. They are omnivores.

### Florida Red-Bellied Turtle (*Pseudemys nelsoni*)

Very similar to the Red-Eared slider in habits and care, the Florida Red-Bellied turtle is found in Georgia and Florida, where he is often seen basking on logs or rocks. The belly isn't really red, but is often splotched with red markings.

The Red-Bellied turtle is not as common among reptile dealers, but is sometimes available as captive bred. These turtles will happily share a tank with Sliders and Painted turtles. Red-Bellied turtles are a bit larger than Sliders or Painted turtles. They require a basking area, and, like many aquatic turtles, are omnivores, growing more herbivorous as they get older.

### Musk Turtle (*Sternotherus odoratus*)

The little Musk turtle, at a length of 4½ inches when full grown, barely reaches the legal size limit for sale in the United States, and is, in fact, one of the smallest turtles in the world. (See chapter 9 for more on the laws that govern pet turtles.)

Don't let the tiny size fool you, though; the Musk turtle is a pugnacious little creature who betrays, in his appearance and his behavior, his close kinship with Snapping turtles. When first captured, Musk turtles will try to bite with a ferocity that belies their tiny size. They will also void the contents of their anal glands, demonstrating why they bear the nickname Stinkpot.

> **TIP**
>
> Many aquatic turtles do not live their entire lives in water, so your tank setup will have to include some basking areas or areas of dry land.

Musk turtles are now captive-red for the pet trade, and settle down to be hardy and active pets. They are capable of asserting themselves even in the company of much larger turtles.

Musk turtles are one of the few turtles who can live in a true aquarium—all water with no land area to crawl out on. They will get along

*Musk turtles are small but assertive.*

quite happily in a bare tank with nothing but several inches of water and a rock cave at the bottom to sleep in.

Musk turtles are carnivores and do not eat much plant material. In the wild they are primarily scavengers and eat dead fish.

## Mud Turtle (*Kinosternon subrubrum*)

The Mud turtle is a close relative of the Musk turtle and is sometimes found on dealers' lists. They grow an inch or two larger than Musk turtles, but can be cared for in the same way.

Like Musk turtles, they do not need a basking area and will live happily in a bare tank with just water, filled as deep as the turtle's shell is long. The Mud turtle is carnivorous, eating carrion and occasionally snapping up a passing fish.

*Mud turtles are meat eaters and will enjoy an occasional meal of fish.*

## Matamata (*Chelus fimbriatus*)

The Matamata is one of the very few Pleurodiran turtles found in the pet trade. In appearance, the Matamata looks convincingly like a large, moss-covered, rotted tree stump. His triangular head has an assortment of wavy frills and fringes, and the carapace is crisscrossed with a number of large, wavy ridges.

The entire turtle is nearly always covered with a thick layer of algae, which gives him a rather unkempt appearance. The algae covering is camouflage, because the Matamata is entirely aquatic and hunts by ambush. When an unsuspecting fish happens by, the Matamata strikes suddenly with his long, snakelike neck and impossibly large mouth.

*Matamatas are among the few side-necked turtles available as pets. The unusual head shape helps camouflage this predator.*

The Matamata is a large turtle, reaching lengths of around 18 inches, but is not very active and does not require an especially large tank. Because he is completely aquatic, he does not need any land area in his tank.

This carnivorous turtle will snap up any fish, frog, or small bird that happens to swim within range.

Unfortunately, this fascinating turtle is bred very rarely and may be difficult to find on dealers' lists (and is not cheap if you do find him). Nevertheless, the Matamata makes an interesting and unusual pet.

## Terrestrial Turtles

### Asian Box Turtle (*Cuora amboinensis*)

These mahogany-color turtles are imported from Southeast Asia, where they spend nearly all their time wallowing about in rice paddies and shallow marshes. They are the most water-loving of the land turtles. Like the North American Box turtle, to whom he is not very closely related, the Asian Box turtle is capable of closing himself tightly into his shell to protect himself from predators.

Asian Box turtles are imported in large numbers and are readily available in the pet trade. Nearly all of them are wild-caught and, like most wild-caught turtles, have parasites. Fortunately, more and more of them are becoming available as captive-bred. Captive-bred specimens can be rather expensive, but are healthier and look better than wild-caught imports.

*Many wild-caught Asian Box turtles end up in the pet trade. Make sure the one you buy is captive-bred.*

The Asian Box turtle is an omnivore and eats both plant and animal material. His shell can reach lengths of around 8 inches.

Housing this species is a bit more complicated than others, because Asian Box turtles split their time equally between terrestrial and aquatic habitats. They will therefore need a large tank (at least 20 gallons) that is equally divided into a land area and a water area.

## Redfoot Tortoise (*Geochelone carbonaria*)

The Redfoot tortoise comes from South America. He is commonly bred in captivity, and is one of the most widely available of the terrestrial tortoises available in the pet trade. Other tortoises who are captive-bred and appear on dealer lists are Greek and Leopard tortoises.

As adults, most tortoise species reach shell lengths between 1 and 2 feet, although some species are as small as 5 or 6 inches and others reach several feet. The Redfoot tortoise has an adult shell length of between 12 and 16 inches.

In captivity, this tortoise needs a more humid environment than many other tortoises. He is a herbivore.

The Redfoot tortoise is a placid and gentle creature who soon becomes a responsive and intelligent pet. Along with the closely related Yellowfoot tortoise (*Geochelone denticulata*), he is one of the best choices for beginning tortoise keepers. The Redfoot likes a heavily planted enclosure with a basking spot and a dish of water to soak in. He is primarily a herbivore.

*An adult Redfoot tortoise can be more than a foot long.*

## Bell's Hingeback Tortoise (*Kinixys belliana*)

These midsize tortoises are native to parts of Africa and Madagascar. The Hingeback is capable of partially closing himself into his shell, but, unlike Box turtles, who have their hinges across the plastron, the Hingeback's shell closes along a joint that runs across the back of the carapace. Curiously, young Hingebacks do not have a functional hinge—the carapace joint only becomes functional after the turtle is several years old.

Hingebacks are one of the medium-size tortoise species; adults will have a shell about 10 inches long. They are omnivores—much more omnivorous than other tortoises—and in addition to eating plants, they will catch insects and other invertebrates.

*Hingebacks eat plants and insects.*

The Bell's Hingeback inhabit savannah grassland with scattered trees. The closely related Forest Hingeback tortoise comes from more heavily forested areas, and is also sometimes seen on dealers' lists. He requires somewhat more humid conditions than his savannah cousin. Hingeback tortoises prefer to be in the shade and don't like bright lighting.

### Russian Tortoise (*Testudo horsefieldi*)

One of the smaller tortoise species, with an adult shell length of 6 to 9 inches, Russian tortoises are native to the arid steppes of Asia, from China to Uzbekistan. They were once imported from Russia by the thousands, but today they are widely available as captive-breds.

*Russian tortoises have a friendly disposition and do well in small groups.*

Their small size, hardiness, and friendly disposition make them well-suited for beginning turtle keepers. In fact, they do well in small groups. This herbivore does not fare well in humid or damp conditions.

Male Russian tortoises are often aggressive toward each other, and generally won't tolerate the presence of another male in their enclosure.

## The Worst Turtles for Beginners

Topping the list is any turtle who is wild-caught. As the number of people enjoying the hobby of turtle-keeping has grown, so, too, have the pressures exerted upon native populations of turtles by collectors who capture wild reptiles for the pet trade. This adds to the already crushing problems of loss of habitat and environmental pollution. As a result, the populations of many species of turtles have plummeted drastically.

It is best for all beginning turtle keepers to restrict themselves to the widely available captive-bred species until they have enough experience and know-how to properly care for the rarer, wild-caught animals. Even the most experienced of

## Multiple Turtles

Once the turtle-keeping bug has bitten you, you will probably want to keep more than one turtle. But before you get another turtle, keep a few things in mind.

Turtles require a large amount of space for housing, and even the smallest of turtle colonies will require a huge amount of room. Most of the active aquatic turtles require at least twenty to thirty gallons of water per adult turtle. So keeping an adult Red-Eared Slider along with a Painted turtle or Red-Bellied turtle will require a tank that holds at least fifty-five gallons. And, since keeping more than one turtle in a tank produces much more mess, you will need a very efficient filtering system.

Keeping more than one adult tortoise is pretty much out of the question unless you keep the very smallest of species (Russian or Hingeback tortoises) or have the space outside to construct a suitable tortoise pen (this will also require that you live in a geographic area that has a suitable climate year-round).

Also keep in mind that you cannot mix turtles or tortoises from different ecological areas or habitats. For instance, keeping a desert tortoise in the same enclosure as a tropical forest tortoise, who requires different temperature and humidity, is a recipe for disaster.

So the general rule for most beginning turtle keepers is one turtle at a time.

turtle keepers, though, should seek out and obtain captive-bred turtles whenever possible, and should make every effort to avoid collecting any specimens of any species who have been taken from the wild.

### Baby Turtles

Baby turtles can be found in virtually every pet store. They are irresistibly cute and inexpensive. They are, however, a poor choice for beginning turtle-keepers.

*Baby Red-Eared Sliders are adorable, but they are very delicate and many die before their first birthday.*

Hatchling turtles are very delicate and require exacting environmental conditions, and also need a demanding diet if they are to avoid serious health problems. Nearly all the hatchling turtles sold in the United States do not live to see their first birthday. It is best for beginners to avoid baby turtles and to obtain well-established adult turtles instead. Since turtles live very long lives, your adult pet will still be with you for many decades.

## North American Box Turtles (*Terrapene carolina*)

North American box turtles, such as the Three-Toed and Gulf Coast Box turtles, were once common in the pet trade and could be found in almost every pet shop. Unfortunately, they are much less commonly seen today than they were a few years ago—a result of their declining populations in the wild due to over-collection and habitat destruction.

*Although they can make good pets, many types of North American Box turtles are endangered. Since they are rarely captive-bred, keeping them as pets only further depletes their dwindling numbers.*

They were recently added to the Convention on the International Trade in Endangered Species (CITES) treaty as a "threatened" species, and their export is now legally regulated. (For more about CITES, see chapter 9.)

Although they make wonderfully responsive pets, Box turtles are only rarely captive-bred and nearly all of the individuals found in the pet trade are taken from the wild. As a result, I strongly encourage you to avoid these species.

## Snapping Turtle (*Chelydra serpentina*)

This prehistoric-looking creature is common throughout most of the eastern and central United States. Although Snapping turtles are very large and can grow up to 18 inches long and weigh more than 40 pounds, they are not active animals and can live comfortably in a relatively small tank. They are very tough and can survive in environmental conditions that would kill most other turtles.

As the name suggests, however, adults are extremely aggressive and never become tame. Baby turtles are not usually as aggressive—but they inevitably grow into adults. Although the power of their bite has been greatly exaggerated in popular myth (no Snapping turtle alive is capable of biting a broomstick in half), large adults are quite

*Snapping turtles are big and aggressive.*

capable of removing fingers and can inflict nasty wounds. This is not an animal anyone would want to keep as a pet.

## Alligator Snapping Turtle (*Macroclemys temmincki*)

These ferocious-looking turtles are the largest species found in North America and the largest freshwater turtle in the world—they can reach lengths up to 3 feet and weigh more than 250 pounds.

Although they have massively muscled jaws and can inflict horrible bites, they are not usually aggressive. However, housing such an enormous turtle is a task that is best left to an aquarium or a zoo rather than a private home. Alligator Snappers are, unfortunately, widely available as captive-bred juveniles.

## Softshell Turtles (*Trionyx* species)

Softshell turtles are a widespread family that is found virtually throughout the world. They are large turtles—up to 18 inches in carapace length—and are interesting animals with several unique adaptations. They are almost entirely aquatic, and have powerful webbed feet for swimming, but they prefer shallow water

*Alligator Snapping turtles are widely available as captive-bred youngsters, but they grow to be 3 feet long and weigh more than 250 pounds!*

*Softshell turtles sicken easily and can be aggressive.*

where they can rest on the bottom occasionally extending their long necks to the surface to breathe through their elongated snorkel-like nose.

As the name suggests, the carapace is leathery and lacks the bony plates found in other turtles, an adaptation that reduces drag while swimming and also flattens the shell, making it easier for the turtle to bury himself in the sandy river bottom to wait for fish and other prey.

Despite their interesting habits and unusual appearance, Softshell turtles are not suitable as pets. Although they are for the most part very shy and prefer to bury themselves placidly at the bottom of their tank, they can be aggressive if threatened and are capable of biting. With their long, snakelike necks and their quick, powerful legs, they have a much longer reach than most other turtles and must be handled carefully. They are also very sensitive to water conditions and very prone to shell infections. They are best left to experienced turtle keepers.

## Diamondback Terrapin (*Malaclemmys terrapin*)

This attractively colored turtle, with his striking black, gray, and white pattern, was once widely found along the Atlantic coast in salt marshes and estuaries. Unfortunately for his well-being, the Diamondback terrapin has a delicately flavored flesh that is highly prized for turtle soups. Although some unsuccessful efforts were made to commercially farm these animals for food, they were hunted almost to extinction for the food trade, and are now listed in several states as endangered or threatened.

*Because they make tasty soup, Diamondback terrapins have been pushed to the brink of extinction.*

In addition to his rarity, the very specialized habitat requirements of the Diamondback terrapin make him unsuitable for most turtle keepers. Diamondbacks are one of the few turtles who have adapted to tolerate brackish or salty water, and they do not do as well when kept in fresh water with other turtles.

## Sulcata or Spurred Tortoise (*Geochelone sulcata*)

These large tortoises are native to the arid grasslands of sub-Saharan Africa. They are the largest tortoises found in Africa, and one of the largest in the world—only the Galapagos and Aldabra Giant tortoises get larger. An adult Sulcata tortoise can have a shell length of 2½ feet and weigh well over 200 pounds.

Although Sulcata tortoises are readily available in the pet trade and are widely captive-bred, their huge size and spacious housing requirements mean they are not a good choice for beginning turtle keepers. Once you have some turtle-keeping experience (and have lots of extra space), they can be viewed as the "holy grail" to which any serious tortoise keeper might aspire.

*Captive-bred Sulcatas are easy to find, but they grow to more than 200 pounds.*

## Chapter 4

# Choosing Your Turtle

**O**nce you've decided what kind of turtle you'd like, the next step is finding somebody who has one to sell. Try to find a source who only sells captive-bred turtles. One of the chief threats facing many wild populations of turtles worldwide is overcollection for the pet trade. You can do your part for turtle conservation by asking where the turtle you are thinking of buying has come from. (For more about turtle conservation, see chapter 9.)

## Where to Get Your Turtle

There are three basic sources for a pet turtle: local breeders or collectors, a mail-order breeder or wholesaler, and local pet shops.

### Breeders

One of the best places to get a pet turtle is from a local breeder or collector—a person who breeds a small number of turtles as a hobby. The advantages are numerous: Most noncommercial, local turtle breeders are very conscientious about their animals and take extraordinary care in keeping and caring for them. (If they didn't, they would have no young turtles to sell.) Since the breeder has a wealth of experience in keeping and raising this species, they will be able to answer any questions you have and pass on useful information and tips on caring for your turtle. (I have met very few turtle breeders who did not relish the chance to help out a beginner.) Price-wise, most noncommercial private breeders are competitive with mail-order dealers, without the shipping costs.

There are a few disadvantages as well, and they must be carefully considered. The biggest problem in dealing with a noncommercial breeder is finding one. Noncommercial turtle breeders are not nearly as common as hobbyists who breed snakes or lizards. Even if you live in a large city, it is unlikely many turtle breeders will live near you. And, since few local turtle breeders advertise, the only way to find them is through

*Hobby breeders take excellent care of their turtles and enjoy sharing what they know with newcomers. They generally hatch a small number of babies each year.*

word of mouth. Your local herpetological society should be able to direct you to reputable breeders in your area—if there are any.

Another potential problem is variety. Breeding turtles takes a lot of room and some expenditure of money. For this reason, most private breeders tend to specialize in one or, at most, a small number of species. And unless you are fortunate enough to find a person who breeds the species you are looking for, you may be out of luck.

The biggest problem, however, is that breeders prefer to sell their stock as soon as possible after it is hatched. In the United States it is illegal to sell any turtle with a carapace less than 4 inches long. There is an exception made to this rule if the turtle is used for "research purposes"; regardless, a large number of breeders and dealers will sell baby turtles anyway.

## Through the Mail

By far the most variety is available if you get a pet turtle through a mail-order dealer or commercial breeder. For some of the more exotic turtles, this may be the only source of that species. Breeders can be found through local herpetological societies, and commercial dealers can be found on the Internet by doing a search for the keywords "turtle breeder" or "turtle prices."

The first step in obtaining a turtle by mail order is to decide what species you would like. Then contact the dealer for a price list and to find out if they have the species you want. Since turtles may be sold under several different names in the pet trade, most dealers list the Latin scientific name, and this is the name you should order by to ensure that you get exactly the species you want.

Turtles are hardy creatures, and shipping them is not difficult. Most dealers will place your turtle inside a cloth bag or a plastic container, along with some moistened paper towels or moss to keep her hydrated and as padding to prevent her from being bounced around. This container is then placed inside a shipping

*A healthy turtle will have beautiful, intact scutes with no scars, cracks, or missing areas.*

box, with several inches of newspaper or foam peanuts as insulation and padding, and the shipping box is completely sealed with tape to prevent rapid temperature changes. The box will then be marked "Live Harmless Reptiles."

There is sufficient air inside the box for several weeks, although most turtles reach their destinations within a few days.

You should specifically request that the shipping company require a signature from you upon delivery. This prevents the delivery person from simply leaving the box by your front door, where it may be exposed to direct sunlight and become too hot for your turtle.

When your turtle arrives, she will be a bit disoriented by her trip, so you should remove her gently from the packaging and place her in her enclosure. Make sure she has food and water, and then leave her alone for a few days to adjust to her new surroundings.

## Turtle Buyer's Club

One option to explore if you want to reduce mailing costs is a local turtle-buyer's club, in which several people get together and order a number of turtles, which are shipped as one order. Since the shipping charge is per box, not per turtle, this practice will lower the shipping cost per person and enable everyone to get the turtles they want at a lower cost than if they placed their orders individually. Your local herpetological society can probably help you set this up.

# How to Choose a Healthy Turtle

Always closely examine any turtle for any possible health problems. The first things to look for are any sort of discharge or fluids in the eyes. If the eyes are not clear and bright, or if they are pasted shut, poor nutrition is the problem and you do not want that turtle.

The next thing to check is the nose and mouth. If the turtle is audibly wheezing while she breathes, if she is breathing with her mouth open, or if you see a fluid bubbling or dripping from the nose, reject the turtle immediately. These are all signs of a respiratory infection, which is potentially life-threatening to the turtle.

Carefully examine the turtle's shell and skin. If there are any patches where the scales or scutes are wrinkled or missing, this indicates a burn or scar injury. Injuries to the scutes or the plastron easily become infected and can turn into problems later. Also, check to be sure the shell itself is firm and hard. If it feels thin, or if it gives way easily to pressure from the fingertips, that is a sign that the shell has not properly developed, probably due to a dietary deficiency.

While you are examining the turtle, look at her general behavior and appearance. Individual turtles do have different personalities, and one individual of a species may be shy and retiring, while another may be confident enough to walk around in your hands. Very few species of turtles will actually attempt to bite—with the exception of Snapping turtles. Most turtles will simply pull in their heads and legs when they feel threatened. If your turtle does not come out of her shell after a few minutes, she may be sick or poorly adjusted to captivity. It is probably best to avoid that turtle.

The turtle's body should also look and feel solid, and the turtle should have some weight. The skin on the legs and neck should fit snugly, without any folds or creases. If there are obvious folds or creases in the skin, it means that the turtle hasn't been eating, which may be a sign of further trouble. Since refusing to eat is a symptom of so many health problems, make sure that the turtle you want has been eating regularly and willingly. You may want to ask that the pet shop personnel feed the turtle in front of you before you buy it.

The best way to place an order with a dealer is by telephone. The dealer will need to know what species you want and what airport you would like them shipped to (for an extra charge, you can sometimes have the package delivered right to your door from the airport).

## Pet Stores

One big advantage a local pet store has over a mail-order dealer is that you are able to closely examine the turtles before you buy them. If you are able to find a turtle you want in a pet store, take the opportunity to examine her carefully. Choosing a healthy turtle to begin with will save you a lot of problems, heartache, and expense down the road.

A good pet store should be able to point you to the local herpetological society for help and advice concerning your turtle.

# Quarantine

Because it may take several weeks for the signs of an illness to be visible, it is a good idea to quarantine any new turtle you bring home, particularly if you already have other turtles or reptiles. Quarantining is simply isolating the new turtle for a period of time so that any potential health problems can be seen and treated. Even if this is your first turtle, you should not skip the quarantine—it is necessary to watch for signs of any impending illness.

*New turtles should be quarantined for a month before they are allowed to mix with your other turtles.*

## Your Quarantine Tank

This tank should be designed for functionality rather than attractiveness. For a land turtle, a 10- or 20-gallon aquarium (depending on the size of the turtle) with newspaper substrate, a water dish, a heating lamp, and an ultraviolet light will do. Aquatic turtles need a water-filled tank (containing no substrate), with a dry basking spot and full-spectrum ultraviolet lighting.

The quarantine tank should be in a separate room from the rest of your reptile collection. Whenever you service your turtle tanks for feeding, cleaning, and other tasks, always do the quarantine tank last to avoid carrying pathogens or parasites from one cage to the next. It may also be helpful to keep the temperature in the quarantine tank a few degrees higher than normal.

Keep a close eye on your new turtle for at least thirty days, keeping in mind all of the potential danger signals mentioned in the box on page 45. If you have a land turtle, be sure to examine her feces whenever they appear. If the feces are loose or watery, if they begin to develop a greenish color, or if the feces begin to take on a strong, unpleasant odor, this may indicate intestinal troubles. Also, if the feces contain a number of thin objects that look like pieces of thread, these are worms, and they will need to be treated by a veterinarian (see chapter 7).

In addition to the normal quarantine, new turtles should be given a routine checkup by a veterinarian, including a fecal exam.

Most turtles who are sick will usually begin to show symptoms within thirty to forty-five days. Some turtle keepers, particularly those with large collections, like to keep their new arrivals quarantined for at least sixty days, because once a disease or parasite has been introduced into a large collection, it is very difficult to contain and control.

If, at the end of the quarantine period, your turtle is still healthy, active and eating regularly, you can move her into her regular home. After removing the turtle, the entire quarantine cage and all of its contents should be emptied and cleaned with a strong saltwater solution or a disinfectant, followed by a thorough rinsing. Do not use any cleanser that contains pine oil or pine tar, because they are very toxic to turtles.

# If Things Don't Work Out

At this point, I must introduce an unpleasant topic. It's a fact that many peopl buy a turtle on impulse and, after they have had her for awhile, lose interest. C people move and their new situation does not enable them to keep their turtl For all of these reasons, it may become necessary to give up your turtle, and w must examine the options you have if you must find your animal a new home.

## What to Do

One good option is to check with your local herpetological society. Many of th larger herp societies have adoption programs that can place unwanted (or con fiscated) reptiles with new owners. The society may be able to find a new hom for your turtle with someone who can demonstrate that they are able to giv them a good home and care for them properly.

The final option, and the one most people turn to first, is to place an ad i the newspaper and sell your turtle. If you choose to do this, be selective abou who you sell the turtle to, particularly if it is a rare or unusual specimen. Do nc sell your turtle to anyone who is not capable of providing proper care.

## What Not to Do

One option that you can rule out right away is donating your turtle to the loca zoo, unless it is a very small zoo with a limited collection (and a limited budget Most of the larger zoos have strict policies against accepting any turtles from pr vate owners, unless the turtle is in exceptional health and of a particularly rar species.

Another option that must be ruled out (but, unfortunately, many times i not) is releasing your turtle into the wild. You may believe that you are doin your turtle a favor by releasing her to wander freely in the great outdoors, but i reality you are probably sentencing the animal to death, perhaps a slow, linge ing one. If your turtle is a tropical species and you live in a temperate or sub tropical area, the first snap of cold weather will probably kill her. If your turtle able to tolerate the local climatic conditions but is not a native species, she ma not be able to find a suitable food source in the wild, and may not be able t compete for resources with the native populations.

Conversely, and more dangerously, the turtle may be able to compete to well, and may be able to establish a breeding population that will crowd out th local species. For example, the Red-Eared Slider has become known as th Reptilian Norway Rat because of her widespread introduction to areas wher she is not native.

*So many Red-Eared Sliders have been turned loose in wild areas that they threaten the native species. Pet turtles belong in homes, not in wild areas.*

In addition, by releasing a captive turtle into the wild, even if she is a native species, you may not only be endangering the life of that particular turtle, but possibly the lives of every other turtle in the area. Turtles who have been kept in pet stores or in collections with other turtles have been exposed to a wide variety of exotic diseases from all over the world. Although many turtles will be killed by these diseases, some will not, and will carry the malignant germs inside their bodies. If these turtles are then released into the wild, they can touch off an epidemic that can decimate the local reptile populations.

For these reasons, no one should ever abandon any pet turtle into the wild. Not only is this practice thoughtless and dangerous, but in many jurisdictions, introducing non-native wildlife is illegal and will be treated as a criminal offense. In fact, because of the danger of spreading disease and parasites, in some states it is illegal to release any captive animal, native or not.

## Chapter 5

# Housing Your Turtle

**H**ousing for turtles depends on the species. Terrestrial turtles, such as the various species of tortoises, require setups similar to those used for snakes and lizards. Aquatic turtles have special requirements of their own. We must therefore consider the housing needs of both categories of turtles separately.

## Terrestrial Turtles

For the smaller terrestrial turtles, such as baby tortoises, the most practical accommodation is an ordinary tropical fish aquarium. Any pet supply store will have a large assortment of aquariums, with several at very inexpensive prices. Glass or plexiglass aquariums are both suitable, but be aware that turtle claws can easily scratch plexiglass, which will cloud the tank walls over time and make it more and more difficult to see your turtle.

By checking the classified ads in the local newspaper, you can usually find a number of aquariums for sale at prices far below those you would pay in a pet supply store. Since you will need a very large tank, buying it through a classified ad is probably the least expensive option. And, since you will not be filling your tank with water, it does not matter if your aquarium leaks (you might even be able to find a pet supply store that has a cracked or leaky tank that they will let you have at cost).

## Size Matters

Many people seem to think that a turtle's size and growth can be limited if he is kept in a smaller tank, or that a turtle will not grow larger than his tank will allow. This is not true. Turtles, like all reptiles, grow throughout their lives. Keeping your turtle in a smaller tank will not limit his growth—it will only ensure that he becomes cramped and unhealthy. For this reason, it is best to provide a tank large enough for your turtle to grow into.

Keep in mind, however, that most species of tortoise will outgrow even the largest of aquariums in just a few years.

## Indoor Tanks

Get the largest tank you possibly can. Terrestrial turtles are, on average, much larger than their aquatic cousins, and being fairly active animals, they require more room to move around than do amphibious turtles. The minimum-size tank for a small Russian tortoise-size terrestrial turtle is 20 gallons, and larger is definitely better. Large tortoises, such as Leopards, Greeks, and Redfoots, require even larger tanks.

Most aquariums come in two styles: the high or show tank, which is designed to be taller than normal; and the low or breeder tank, which has lower sides but a wider bottom area. Since turtles cannot climb the glass, high sides are not

*Get the biggest tank you can. Low sides are okay—it's the surface area on the bottom that counts.*

necessary, and the breeder style of tank provides the maximum area usable by the turtle.

Unless you will be adding a lid, the tank should be a minimum of several inches taller than the turtle is long. If the sides are too low, the turtle will be able to hook his front claws on the edge and pull himself up and out. If you have more than one turtle per tank, or if you have rocks or tree branches for decoration, keep in mind that these can all serve as ladders for an escape attempt. For maximum security, the sides of the tank should be as high as is practical for you to still reach inside and easily clean, feed, and tend your turtle.

As long as your turtle cannot get up the sides of the tank, you will not need a lid to keep him in. However, if you have cats, dogs, or small children, you may need a screened lid to keep them out. Several types of screen lids are available for most aquarium sizes, and all are suitable for turtle tanks.

### The Kiddie Pool

Another option used by many tortoise keepers as an enclosure for their young tortoise is a large children's wading pool. These one-piece plastic pools come in a variety of sizes and depths. They are placed in a suitable area, lined with a suitable substrate, and serve as practical enclosures for young tortoises.

## Outdoor Turtle Pen

Another option for the serious turtle keeper is to build an outdoor turtle pen. For adult tortoises of most species, this is pretty much the only suitable option. This project is most satisfying in areas where the climate allows the turtles to be kept outside permanently; in most areas of the United States, winter conditions necessitate bringing the turtles inside in the cold weather. If you keep turtles native to your area, however, they can hibernate naturally right inside their pen.

Most tortoises do not hibernate, so they can only be kept outdoors in the southern regions of the United States, where their natural environmental conditions can be approximated. Keep in mind that heat is not the only consideration: Tropical tortoises such as Redfoots won't do well in arid areas like Arizona, while desert tortoises such as Sulcatas won't do well in humid areas like Florida.

The pen should be as large as is practical, and should contain areas of shade and areas of sun. It is very important that the turtle pen have at least some areas of shade at all times during the day, because unprotected tortoises can overheat quickly in a full midday sun. At the same time, warm basking spots must always be available. Tortoises should be able to regulate their body temperature by moving from sun to shade as needed.

Several large, flat rocks can serve as basking spots and will retain heat. You will also need some rock caves where the turtles can retreat for shade and whenever

*Big adult tortoises will do well in a large outdoor pen. Consider the climate in your area and in your tortoise's natural habitat before you get a species that will end up living outside.*

they need to feel secure. If the bulk of the pen area is left in its natural state, with several inches of soil, some leaf litter, and vegetation, the turtles will spend most of their time happily digging and foraging for edible plants.

Your turtles will require water, and many terrestrial tortoises do like an occasional soaking, so the turtle pen should also contain a small, shallow pond. Since terrestrial tortoises do not swim well and can drown quite easily, the water should be just barely deep enough to cover the turtle's legs.

The pond will lose water steadily to evaporation and will have to be topped up often. It will also be soiled with dirt and leaf litter by the turtle, and will have to be emptied, cleaned, and refilled occasionally—a menial but vital task.

Make sure there are no toxic plants anywhere in the enclosure. Common plants that are dangerous to turtles include:

| | |
|---|---|
| Azalea | Philodendron |
| Belladonna | Rhododendron |
| Daffodil | Snapdragon |
| Elderberry | Tulip |
| Horse chestnut | Wisteria |
| Larkspur | Yew |

The perimeter of the turtle pen can be made from wooden planks, bricks, or stones. The wall must be at least several inches higher than the length of the longest turtle you will be keeping. If you make the wall just high enough that you can step over it, the turtles will be prevented from climbing out and you will be spared the necessity of making a gate for the pen. If you are keeping Wood turtles or other good climbers, it's best to have an overhanging lip around the inside top of the wall to prevent escape. Large tortoises such as Sulcatas, on the other hand, are like living tanks, and can plow right through a flimsy fence.

Since tortoises are excellent diggers, you will need some way to discourage your pets from tunneling to freedom. The best way to prevent escapes is to build the entire turtle pen from wood or stone, including a full floor, and then filling in the pen with a foot or two of topsoil before landscaping it. Burrowers can then tunnel to their heart's content without being able to get out. Another method (which is less expensive and requires a lot less work) is to sink the walls of the pen a foot or so into the ground. Although the turtles may repeatedly attempt to dig their way underneath the fence, eventually they will tire and give up.

If you intend to keep the turtles in their pen year-round, there must be enough dirt and leaf litter for the turtles to get beneath the frost line so they can hibernate in winter (more on that later in this chapter).

If you live in a rural area, it is possible that your turtle pen will attract natural predators such as raccoons or foxes. If it becomes necessary to protect your

*If your outdoor turtles are hibernating, they will need a deep substrate of leaf litter to dig beneath.*

turtles from these predators, you can string some wire mesh screen over the top of the entire pen, from wall to wall.

## Substrates

A wide variety of materials can be used as the substrate for an indoor turtle tank. Each has advantages and disadvantages, and each has advocates and detractors among reptile keepers.

### Newspaper

The most functional and economical lining is ordinary newspaper. This can be cut to size and placed in the tank, three or four layers thick, and is easily cleaned by simply removing the old paper and replacing it with fresh sheets. Because newspaper is fairly absorbent and turtle droppings do not contain much moisture, it is unlikely that there will be any problem with waste soaking through to the tank floor. A newspaper substrate also makes it easy to spot parasites, as well as changes in the turtle's feces. And newspaper substrate is plentiful, easily obtained and costs next to nothing.

The disadvantage to a tank lined with newspaper is its rather sterile appearance. It just doesn't look natural. If you would like a more natural appearance for your turtle's tank (it makes no difference whatsoever to the turtle), then you will need to use some other substrate.

### Natural Substrates

Shredded tree bark or something similar is a natural option. Among the substances offered for sale are orchid bark, aspen wood chips (*not* wood shavings), cocoa bean shells, and ground-up corn cobs. Some keepers will use ordinary rabbit pellets as a safe substitute. These materials are relatively inexpensive, absorbent, and easy to clean—simply scoop out the feces and replace a handful of the substrate. Turtles also like them because they get to dig around in the pellets.

One disadvantage of shredded tree bark is that if you are feeding your turtle slimy prey such as worms, or wet or sticky foods such as fruits, pieces of the substrate will stick to the food and be swallowed by the turtle. This can cause serious health problems. Another big disadvantage is that most of these materials tend to get moldy and begin to rot if they get wet from the turtle's droppings or from water splashed from the turtle's dish. These substrates must be cleaned nearly every day, and the soiled spots replaced with a bit of fresh material.

Desert turtles, such as some tortoises, can have a substrate consisting of several inches of clean sand. The drawback of sand is that it is not very absorbent and will have to be cleaned rather often.

*Rabbit pellets make a great substrate. They're easy to keep clean and the turtles like to dig in them.*

## Aquarium Gravel

Most of the prepackaged turtle kits you can find in a pet supply shop use ordinary aquarium gravel as a substrate. Although gravel is a workable substrate for tortoises, it has fallen out of favor because of the danger that it can be swallowed by the turtle and can cause severe intestinal blockage. Gravel is not absorbent, either, and can be difficult to keep clean unless it is either replaced often or periodically removed, rinsed, and dried.

## AstroTurf

The most popular substrate is a sheet of the artificial grass known as AstroTurf. This material comes in single, presized sheets that fit inside a standard aquarium, where it lies on the bottom like a carpet. Sold in hardware stores, garden stores, and pet supply stores, AstroTurf is attractive, relatively inexpensive, and easy to use.

However, this substrate has two disadvantages. First, its edges are usually rough-cut, with small plastic strings that continually unravel from the edges. These strings present severe problems if accidentally swallowed by the turtle. One solution is to buy a sheet of AstroTurf that is slightly larger than the bottom of the tank, and, using a needle and fishing line, fold the edges under and sew them down, like a hem. This prevents the strings of plastic from unraveling.

Another disadvantage to AstroTurf is that because it is plastic, it is not absorbent and requires frequent cleaning. This entails dismantling all the tank

## Substrates to Avoid

Definitely avoid pine and cedar shavings, such as those sold for mice and hamsters. The small particles of dust produced by these shavings are very irritating to a turtle's lungs and mouth, and the volatile oils in the wood (particularly in cedar) can be very toxic to turtles.

"Natural" tanks, which use a layer of soil with live plants as a substrate, should also be avoided. They are difficult to clean and maintain, and turtles tend to dig into the substrate, uprooting the plants and quickly destroying the setup.

furnishings and removing the liner. Most turtle keepers who use AstroTurf will use two sheets, so they can place one sheet in the tank while the other is being cleaned.

## Keeping Your Turtle Warm

Because turtles are ectotherms and cannot produce their own body heat, they must be provided with outside heat sources to maintain their optimum body temperature. This is the most crucial factor in successfully keeping reptiles in captivity—nearly every health problem turtles face can be directly traced to how well their thermal requirements are being met.

Heat can be thought of as fuel—the higher the temperature, the faster the turtle's metabolism becomes, and the more efficiently he can move, digest food, resist disease, and perform other biological functions.

Tortoises are also very susceptible to respiratory infections if they are kept in conditions that are too chilly or drafty, even for a short period of time. They must be kept warm if they are to remain healthy.

### Different Temperature Requirements

No one single temperature is best for keeping all turtles. Turtles from different regions and natural habitats require different ranges of temperatures.

Specific temperature requirements for individual turtles will vary depending upon the turtle's biological activity. That's why you must provide a range of different temperatures, or a temperature gradient, that enables the turtle to select the temperature he wants by moving from warmer to cooler areas.

*Among other problems, most turtles will not eat if they are too hot or too cold.*

The electric hot rocks or sizzle stones that are often sold in pet supply stores should not be used in any turtle's tank. The inability to regulate their temperature, malfunctions, and risk of burns make them problematic. Hot rocks do not warm the surrounding air very much, and the only way for the turtle to obtain the heat is through physical contact with the heater. Since turtles have few nerve endings in their plastrons, it is not at all rare for them to sit on an overheated hot rock, unaware that their skin is being severely burned. Sizzle stones are also useless in providing a workable temperature gradient and do not allow the turtle to effectively thermoregulate. Finally, hot rocks do not allow turtles to mimic their natural behavior patterns, since the majority of turtles obtain most of their heat by basking in strong sunlight rather than by contact with a heated surface. Most turtles prefer that their heat source come from above.

It may seem to be a simple matter to place the turtle's tank near a window, where it will receive warmth from direct sunlight. However, in an enclosed aquarium, direct sunlight would quickly trap the heat and raise the temperature to lethal levels. You'll need heat sources you can regulate.

### Basking Lamps

Using an incandescent basking lamp is one way to safely duplicate the warming effects of the sun. (This must, however, be supplemented with full-spectrum lighting—more on this later.) The size, power, and distance above the tank of the basking lamp must be determined through trial and error, and will depend upon the temperature range desired as well as the size and dimensions of the tank. In other words, you'll have to place a thermometer on the bottom of the tank and take a variety of temperature readings over several hours.

For most terrestrial tortoises, the temperature directly under the basking light should be in the 90- to 95-degree range, while the temperature at the far end of the tank should be around 80 degrees. In most tanks, a 75-watt spotlight bulb provides adequate heat. Place the basking lamp in a spot where it cannot be reached or physically touched by the turtle, since contact can produce serious burns.

Recently, a ceramic heating element that replaces incandescent basking lights has come on the market. It uses a heat bulb and a socket that resembles a light bulb, but gives off only heat without light. Ceramic elements can be connected to small thermostats for precise heat control—which also makes them much more expensive than ordinary basking lights.

For best results, the turtle tank should have ceramic heating elements to produce a hot spot for basking, and a full-spectrum fluorescent light to provide ultraviolet wavelengths. Both should be wired to an electric timer, and the heater should be controlled with a thermostat. This setup is suitable for any terrestrial turtle.

## Warming the Substrate

Certain turtles, including the Greek and Leopard tortoise, require additional "belly heat" from an artificially warmed substrate to aid in digestion. Since electric hot rocks and heated plastic hide boxes can be dangerous, I recommend using one of two other sources.

One, the undertank heater, is like a tiny heating pad or electric blanket. It is placed underneath the turtle tank, where it produces heat that diffuses through the floor of the tank and substrate.

The other, heat tape, is similar, but comes in a long electric ribbon that fastens to the bottom of the tank. Both produce enough heat to penetrate half-inch plywood and produce temperatures in the low 80s. Both are rather expensive, however.

> **T I P**
>
> Every turtle tank should contain at least one thermometer to monitor the temperature. The stick-on thermometers used in tropical fish tanks work well and are inexpensive. Some turtle keepers like to have two thermometers—one at the warm end and one at the cool end of the tank.

## Light

Turtles have internal body clocks that respond to changes in light, and thus need a cycle of light and dark to keep all their internal processes in sync.

Proper lighting is also important for efficient vitamin absorption. Tortoises, like most reptiles, cannot store vitamin D3 in their bodies, and so use the ultraviolet wavelengths found in natural sunlight to manufacture this vitamin in their skin. Vitamin D3 is necessary to help your turtle use the calcium in his food to produce new bone tissue. Without a source of ultraviolet light to activate D3, turtles will suffer from nutritional deficiencies and die. They therefore need exposure to natural, unfiltered sunlight or to special full-spectrum lamps that duplicate the ultraviolet wavelengths found in natural sunlight.

## Ultraviolet Light Requirements

Since there is no accepted standard definition of "full-spectrum" lighting, you must be cautious in selecting a light for your turtle habitat. Some companies use "full-spectrum" to refer to the presence of *any* ultraviolet (UV) light. The artificial sunlamps used for indoor plants fall into this category.

There are two types of ultraviolet rays: UV-A and UV-B. Plants need large amounts of UV-A, and these are the wavelengths that are found in indoor grow lights. Reptiles need UV-B wavelengths to synthesize vitamin D3; therefore, they need a full-spectrum lamp specifically designed for reptiles, which emits a large amount of UV-B light. The best advice for beginners is to stick with the full-spectrum UV-B fluorescent lamps to meet your reptile's needs.

The UV lamp must be as close as practical to your turtles, keeping in mind that both glass and clear plastic filter out nearly all the ultraviolet wavelengths. Shine the UV lamp directly onto your turtles, with no intervening glass or plastic. Since UV bulbs lose energy with age, they should be replaced every six months.

*Terrestrial turtles should be exposed to as much unfiltered natural sunlight as possible.*

## Sunlight

Terrestrial turtles should also be exposed to as much unfiltered natural sunlight as possible. According to some estimates, a turtle gets more useful UV-B in fifteen minutes of exposure to natural sunlight than he does in several hours of exposure to artificial UV light. Remember that sunlight coming in through window glass is not unfiltered, and will not give your turtle the light he needs.

## Lighting Hood

Recently, special lighting hoods that contain both an incandescent heat bulb and a fluorescent full-spectrum lamp in one fixture have become available. These two-in-one fixtures enable you to connect both basking heat and ultraviolet light to a single outlet. They are suitable for any terrestrial turtle's tank.

### Lighting Schedules

To duplicate the natural environment as closely as possible, turtles from equatorial or tropical areas should have a twelve-hour-on, twelve-hour-off light schedule, which mimics the length of the tropical day. Temperate turtles can also tolerate a tropical light schedule; however, it is best to mimic the natural length of the day, making the light period shorter in winter and longer in summer.

# Hide Box

Turtles are well-protected against predators inside their bony shells, but they prefer to have a dark retreat where they can hide and feel safe. They also need an area of shade where they can avoid overheating. For these reasons, all terrestrial turtles need a hide box.

The hide box should be snug, with enough room for the turtle to enter and turn around when he is inside (turtles cannot easily back up if they encounter an

*Every turtle needs a place to hide and cool down.*

obstruction). A wooden box, a little longer on each side than the length of the turtle, with one side removed for an entrance, makes a good hide box. A suitable retreat can also be made using rocks and flat stones to build a shallow cave. The hide box should be placed at the end of the tank opposite the basking spot.

## Tank Furniture

Most tortoises will do quite well in a barren tank with just substrate, a water dish, a hide box, and a heat and light source. Such tanks are rather unattractive, though, and most people want to include some sort of decoration or "furniture" for the turtle tank. These decorations are for your pleasure, not the turtle's. So the main considerations are that they are easy to keep clean and are safe for your reptile.

### Rock Piles

Many turtle keepers like to place a small, flat pile of rocks in the tank to help retain heat from the basking light. Multicolored or unusually shaped rocks for use in fish tanks can be found in aquarium shops or in your backyard. Any rocks used in a turtle tank must be smooth, because sharp or rough edges can injure the turtle's plastron and lead to bacterial or fungal infections.

Rock piles should be low enough that the turtle can easily climb on and off them. Most turtles can right themselves if they accidentally fall onto their backs, but some of the desert tortoises, which have high, domed shells, may not be able to. If they are trapped on their backs under a basking light, they may quickly overheat and die.

To prevent parasites, rocks and stones must be carefully cleaned and disinfected before being placed in the tank. The best way to disinfect them is to soak them overnight in a three-percent solution of ordinary laundry bleach (sodium hypochlorite) or a strong salt solution. This should be enough to kill any bugs hiding within. Afterward, thoroughly wash the rocks in a large amount of water to rinse away any trace of the disinfectant.

> **CAUTION**
>
> Commercial disinfectants that contain pine tar or pine oil are extremely toxic to most reptiles, and should never be used to clean your pet's tank or anything in it.

### Live Plants

Live plants are often used in a tortoise tank to give it a more natural appearance. Plants must be chosen very carefully, since terrestrial tortoises will eat a lot of plant material, some of which is extremely toxic to reptiles. Plants to avoid

*Plants make a tank look more natural, but your turtle is very likely to dig them up and eat them.*

include coleus, crocus, impatiens, poinsettia, Spanish bayonet, trumpet vine, and Virginia creeper.

Even if the plant is safe and will not harm the tortoise, it is a virtual certainty that the tortoise will harm the plant, either by crawling over it and crushing it or by eating all the foliage. In any case, desert tortoises require conditions that are too dry for most live plants, and such tortoises are best kept in a bare tank with just a few rocks. If you'd like, you can arrange some potted cactus plants in the tank, but they will very likely be gnawed on continuously by the tortoises, and will eventually be uprooted and destroyed.

For all these reasons, it is best not to use any plants at all in the tortoise tank. Of course, it is possible to use plastic plants, which won't get eaten and can easily be rearranged after the tortoise has dug them up for the thousandth time. (Take care, though, because some tortoises aren't that bright, and they will try to swallow the plastic plants.)

## Aquatic Turtles

Aquatic turtles need a setup that is similar to that used for aquarium fish. Therefore, the equipment you'll need to house aquatic turtles can be found at any aquarium shop.

## Tank

The first requirement is a tank that is big enough for your turtles. Although the
will spend most of their time basking lazily, aquatic turtles are active swimmer
and need lots of room. Juvenile turtles will need at least a 10-gallon tank. Adul
turtles need a minimum of 20 gallons per turtle. The larger the tank, the bette
It is best to use the low or breeder style of aquariums, since these maximize th
available surface area.

A few turtle species can live in a true aquarium—all water without any lan
to crawl out on. These include Musk and Mud turtles, Softshells, an
Matamatas. Setting up a suitable tank for these species is simplicity itself: A
you need is a tank of suitable size and, for the smaller Mud and Musk turtles, a
underwater rock cave for hiding and sleeping. Adult Mud and Musk turtles wi
have enough space in a 10-gallon tank.

In the wild, Mud and Musk turtles prefer areas with thick, muddy bottom
In captivity, such a setup with substrate at the bottom of the tank, even grave
or stones, traps dirt and detritus and makes it more difficult to keep the tan
clean. This means that despite their preferences, the bottom of the tank shoul
be bare.

*Some aquatic turtles are not great swimmers and should be able to rest on the bottom of their tank and
simply stick their nose up to breathe.*

Ironically, these aquatic species (with the exception of Softshells) are not very good swimmers. They move around by walking along the bottom of the tank, so you must make sure to maintain the water at a proper depth. These species prefer to rest on the bottom of the tank and occasionally extend their nose to the surface, like a snorkel, to breathe. They cannot easily swim to the surface to breathe, and can drown if the water is too deep for them. The water in their tank should therefore be deep enough to cover them completely, but shallow enough to ensure that every turtle can reach the surface with his nose.

The other aquatic turtles are strong swimmers and need a large, deep water area where they can swim and exercise properly. The water should be at least as deep as the shell of the turtle is long, and for strong swimmers, such as Painted Turtles and Sliders, it should be much deeper, allowing plenty of room for swimming and exercise.

## Basking Area

Most aquatic turtles are amphibious and will need a land area in their tank where they can bask and dry off. This is important for both thermoregulation and to prevent a buildup of fungus on the turtle. This basking area should be at one end of the tank and must be big enough to allow all the turtles in the tank

*Make sure your aquatic turtle can easily climb out of the water and onto a dry basking area.*

to bask at the same time, but should not cover more than one-third of the tank area. That means if you have several turtles, you will need quite a large tank.

There are several ways to set up a suitable basking area. Perhaps the easiest is to pile up a number of flat rocks at one end of the tank so they form an underwater cave below and protrude above the surface to provide a dry area for basking. Line this area with a moss substrate to prevent the turtles from injuring their plastrons on sharp edges as they climb on and off the basking platform. Make sure you stack the rocks very securely, so they will not wobble or tilt as the turtles climb on them.

A second alternative is to cut a piece of wood just big enough to fit inside the tank at the water level, and use thin wedges of wood to press it tightly against the sides of the tank to hold it in place. One potential problem with this kind of basking area, however, is that the wood may become waterlogged and swell up, pushing apart the sides of the tank and perhaps causing leaks.

Whatever material you use, it is important that the land tilt gently into and beneath the water surface to allow the turtles to easily climb out. It is very difficult for turtles, especially young ones, to clamber onto a land surface that is above or level with the water, unless there is a submerged section at the shore for them to push off from.

Some hobbyists house their turtles in an aquavivarium, in which one half of the tank is open water and the other is a landscaped dry area, using soil or some other substrate. The land and water areas can be separated by a strip of glass or a clear plastic sheet glued across the tank with silicone aquarium sealer and extending about two-thirds of the way up the sides of the tank. The larger side of the tank is then filled with water, up to the level of the dividing barrier (as in the true aquarium, no substrate should be used in the water area of the tank). The smaller portion is filled with substrate and then landscaped as a natural terrarium. Several flat rocks or pieces of wood are placed to form a ramp so the turtles can climb out of the water. These soil setups, while attractive, are not easy to maintain because they need frequent cleaning. If the soil is covered with a layer of moss, it will help prevent the turtle from dragging dirt into the water.

Aquarium gravel should not be used, because it has sharp edges that will make small cuts in the turtle's plastron and could lead to infection. Rounded river gravel could be used instead, but the rounded pieces will constantly get pushed into the water.

## Heating

The aquatic turtle tank has two separate areas—the water and the dry basking area—and both need to be heated. Each must be considered separately.

The basking area, where the turtles can thermoregulate and dry themselves off, can be heated using the same methods already described for the terrestrial turtle tank—an incandescent basking lamp or a ceramic heating element with a rheostat (a dimmer switch that allows the heat output to be adjusted). For most aquatic turtles, the temperature under the basking spot should be around 85 to 90 degrees Fahrenheit.

## Heating the Water

Some of the northern species of aquatic turtles, such as Musk turtles and Painted turtles, will do fine if the water is kept at ordinary room temperature, so you will not need a heater for the water area of the tank. Other species, however, including Sliders, Reeve's turtles, and Matamatas, require somewhat higher temperatures, and the water portion of their aqua-terrarium must be heated.

The best equipment for this task is the submersible water heater commonly used in tropical fish tanks. This is a glass tube that contains an electrical heating element and a thermostat. It attaches to the lip of the tank and extends into the water. The output of this kind of heater is usually controlled by a small knob or dial at the top. For most aquatic turtles, a water temperature of 75 to 78 degrees Fahrenheit is suitable.

The fragility of these heaters poses a safety problem. Swimming turtles commonly knock the heater against the aquarium glass and crack it, or even attempt to climb up the heater tube and pull the whole thing into the water, presenting a serious electrocution hazard.

To guard against this, turtles must be prevented from physically touching the glass tube. The best way to do this is to

> ### CAUTION
> Undertank heaters and heating tape should not be used in an aquatic turtle's tank, since they can present a serious risk of electrocution (both to the turtles and to you) if the tank leaks even a tiny bit.

surround the heater with a large pile of rocks that allows water to circulate around it while at the same time screening the heater from the turtles. Another method, which can be used if the tank has a large power filter (as indeed it should), is to place the heater in the filter box instead of the main tank, so the heated water flows from the filter back into the aquavivarium. Since most filter cases are made of plastic, though, it is important to make sure the heating element does not touch the plastic, which could melt a hole and cause leaks.

## Lighting

A few species of aquatic turtles do not require any lighting in their tanks—they prefer dark or dimly lit areas. The Matamata, for instance, favors still, murky waters in shady areas, where visibility is poor and sunlight rarely penetrates. These turtles get most of their calcium and vitamin D from their prey, rather than through exposure to sunlight.

Other aquatic turtles, however, require ultraviolet light to properly synthesize vitamin D3, which is necessary for the metabolism of calcium to build shell and bones. This necessary light must be provided with the same sort of full-spectrum UV-B lamps that were described for terrestrial tortoises. Like terrestrial tortoises, aquatic turtles also benefit greatly from small periods of exposure to unfiltered natural sunlight.

The commercial "two-in-one" hoods, which contain both a full-spectrum fluorescent lamp and an incandescent basking bulb, are useful for aquatic tanks since they use only one electrical cord and thus reduce the number of necessary electrical connections.

## Filters

Keeping the aquatic turtle tank clean is extremely important. Dirty tanks with polluted water not only encourage the rapid growth of algae and other pests, but they are unhealthy for the turtles and for you, since they provide perfect breeding grounds for the salmonella organism (see chapter 6 for more on salmonella).

*The Matamata prefers still, murky water with low light, so he can look like a floating leaf and sneak up on prey. But most turtles need full-spectrum ultraviolet light to survive.*

Keeping a turtle tank clean is a challenge that is complicated by the biology of the animals. Aquatic turtles do not excrete on land, and will only void their feces into the water area of their aquarium. Most of the feces is water-soluble urea and ammonia, so cannot simply be scooped out. In addition, if soil or some other substrate is used for the land area of the tank, it will stick to the turtle's shell and feet and will be dragged into the water. Finally, when the turtles are fed in their tank, small bits of uneaten food will remain and decay, releasing toxins and fouling the water.

For these reasons, the water in the turtle tank must be cleaned continuously using powerful filters to clarify and purify the water. A number of such filters are widely available in aquarium supply shops, but most of these have been designed with the needs of fish keepers in mind, not turtle hobbyists. You must therefore be very careful in choosing a filter for your tank.

The most suitable filter for a turtle tank is the power filter, which hangs on the outside of the aquarium and uses an electric motor to pull water into the filter through a long plastic intake tube. After passing through a layer of glass wool and activated charcoal (which cleans and purifies the water), the siphoned water is then returned to the tank through a trough or a plastic outlet.

*Aquatic turtles eliminate only in water, so they are literally swimming in their own toilet. You need a powerful filter to keep the water clean.*

This kind of filter is available in a variety of sizes for different size tanks. The manufacturers produce lists that specify which size filter is suitable for which size tank. However, the lists are calculated on the assumption that the aquarium will contain fish. Turtles, simply put, are much bigger and much dirtier than fish, and require substantially more filtering power. If you have one or two turtles in your tank, you should select the size filter that is recommended for a tank two sizes larger than yours. In other words, if you have a 10-gallon tank, use a filter that is designed for a 20-gallon tank. If you have a larger tank with more turtles, get the largest capacity filter you can. If your tank is very large—more than 55 gallons— you may need to buy two filters and run them both at the same time.

Although such large filters can be rather expensive, turtles kept in clean water are much healthier. Plus, the reduced risk of salmonella for you more than makes up for this initial expense.

### Filter Maintenance

Maintaining a power filter is a simple matter. Most filters use a disposable pad or filter element that slips into place inside the filter box. Once this has become loaded with detritus, you just pull it out and replace it with a fresh one. Your turtle's lifestyle will necessitate frequent replacement of the filter elements.

### Partial Water Changes

No matter how powerful your filter, it is still necessary to periodically remove a portion of the water in the tank and replace it with fresh water. That's because as waste products are excreted into the water, they produce ammonia toxins that filters alone cannot remove.

For most tanks, replacing half the water every four weeks will be sufficient—assuming the turtles are being fed in another container. If you have a turtle who must be fed in his home tank, replace half the tank's water every week.

The replacement water should be at roughly the same temperature as the water being portion. If your local water is heavily chlorinated, it should be allowed to stand in an open container for twenty-four hours so any toxic compounds can dissipate.

## Intake Tube Considerations

Power filters must process large volumes of water at a time, producing a powerful flow of water into the intake tube that can be a potential danger to smaller turtles. Occasionally, a smaller turtle may venture too close to the intake tube and be sucked against the tube by the water pressure, where he will be pinned until he drowns. Plastic intake tubes are also vulnerable to damage by turtles who swim into them or try to climb onto them.

The intake tubes for your filter must be separated from the turtles the same way you protect the water heater. It is best to place the intake tube in a corner of the tank and then surround it with a wall of rocks.

It is important that the intake tube of the filter reach all the way to the bottom of the tank, to siphon up all of the detritus, feces, and uneaten food. Most filters come with plastic extension tubes that enable them to reach all the way to the bottom of the tank.

## Outdoor Turtle Pond

Large colonies of aquatic turtles can be kept outside in an artificial pond—a strategy best suited to areas with warm weather year-round. The basic setup for an aquatic turtle pen is the same as that already described for terrestrial tortoises. You will need to fence or wall in a large outdoor area with a variety of naturally occurring temperatures, including areas of shade and sun. The walls should be as high as practical and should be sunk into the ground to discourage burrowing (however, aquatic turtles are not as proficient diggers as their terrestrial cousins).

The water pond for a colony of aquatic turtles must, of course, be much more extensive than that in the outdoor tortoise pen. A complete artificial pond, with the appropriate vegetation and basking spots, can be installed anywhere there is sufficient room. Dig out an area the size and depth that you want the finished pond to be. A good pond should be a minimum of 10 feet across, with no rocks or other protruding objects left at the bottom of the hole. The center of the pond should be at least 2 feet deep so it won't freeze solid in the winter.

Once you have excavated a suitable hole, line it with a strong waterproof material, such as butyl rubber, as thick as practical to prevent tears. This serves the same function as a swimming pool liner: It prevents leaks, keeps the dirt out of the water, and keeps the pond water from draining away. The liner should overlap the edges of the pond by about a foot, with the overlapping edge covered over by several inches of rocks and soil to hold it firmly in place.

Next, fill the interior of the liner with 4 or 5 inches of clean sand, to push the liner flat against the bottom and protect it from rocks, branches, turtle claws, and other potential sources of puncture. Once the liner is firmly in place, add enough water to fill the pond.

If the pond is large enough—at least 10 feet by 10 feet—and contains a number of aquatic plants, a natural filtration cycle will be established, in which the turtle waste is used by the plants as fertilizer and the plants, in turn, will oxygenate the water. This system removes the necessity for filters or water changes, although the pond may need to be topped up with water during dry periods.

You should plant shallow areas near the shore of a permanent pond with cattails, pickerel weed, and other aquatic plants that provide cover for young turtles and attract insect life to the pond. The turtles can use a number of flat rocks scattered along the shore as entry and exit ramps and as basking spots. Another good idea is to place a large tree branch or trunk in the pond, so it forms a long basking platform that can be reached from either land or water. Most aquatic turtles prefer to bask on logs or branches that extend out into the water so they can dive to safety at the first hint of danger.

The area around the pond should be open and sunny for basking most of the day, with plants and small bushes placed at the margins to provide some shade. Large trees should be avoided, as they shed leaves that would build up in and around the pond.

*If you live in a warm climate, an outdoor turtle pond can be a fascinating ecosystem for your backyard.*

## Chapter 6

# Feeding Your Turtle

**B**ecause turtles are found in a wide variety of habitats, ranging from the open sea to arid deserts, their food preferences are wide ranging. Some turtles are entirely carnivorous; others are largely herbivorous and thrive on plant material.

In general, terrestrial tortoises tend to have different food preferences than aquatic turtles, and in any case the process of feeding a captive land turtle is very different from that of feeding aquatic turtles. For this reason, both types of turtle will be discussed separately.

## Terrestrial Turtles

In the wild, African, European, and Asian tortoises are entirely herbivorous, and graze on grasses, succulents, and other plants. Captive tortoises, such as Sulcatas and Russian tortoises, can be fed a variety of high-fiber, high-calcium plant foods, including grass, hay, and flowers. All captive tortoises enjoy the opportunity to wander around the yard and graze on grass, flowers, and other plants.

South American Redfoot and Yellowfoot tortoises, who come from a wetter and more humid habitat than arid-adapted African tortoises, are a bit more omnivorous, and prefer more fruit and some animal foods in their meals.

Box turtles, in contrast to all tortoises, usually prefer much more meat in their diets. In the wild, they will eat plant food such as berries, mushrooms, and fruits, but a large portion of their diet consists of invertebrates and small animals, including earthworms, snails, and salamanders.

*Turtles will thrive on a varied diet. Interestingly, they seem to consider red foods to be a special treat.*

Most Box turtles will eagerly accept fresh earthworms, either whole or chopped, and many will also take goldfish or snails. Ornate Box turtles, who are native to the dry prairie, consume a lot of beetles and bugs in the wild, and will often accept crickets in captivity, hunting them down one by one and eating them.

All turtles fed live food must be checked regularly for intestinal pests, since raw meat may contain worms and other parasites.

## Supplements

Tortoises, especially youngsters with growing shells, are susceptible to vitamin and mineral deficiencies, so dietary supplements should be regularly added to the tortoise's food. Calcium and vitamin D3 are especially important, because most tortoises are kept indoors, where they cannot get unfiltered exposure to the sunlight that would help them synthesize these essential nutrients. They should therefore be provided with a pinch of phosphorus-free calcium powder (such as RepCal) with every other meal. Another option is to place a piece of cuttlebone (used for birds) in the tortoise's enclosure. The tortoise will nibble on it for the calcium content.

Some keepers also like to provide an occasional multivitamin tablet (crushed and sprinkled over the food) to help prevent vitamin deficiencies.

## Eating Schedules

Like all reptiles, tortoises are capable of incredibly long fasts, and can go a long time between feedings. Most tortoises, however, should be fed daily. If you will be going on vacation for two or three weeks, your tortoise will be fine as long as you give her as much as she will eat before you leave and one good meal when you get back.

In the wild, tortoises tend to be grazers and nibblers. They eat a little bit here and a little bit there as they wander from plant to plant. In captivity, they may also prefer to nibble a little from their food dish, wander around a bit, and then return to nibble some more. Some individual tortoises, though, may prefer to remain at their food dish and eat their fill at one sitting.

In either case, you want to prevent the tortoise's fruits and vegetables from spoiling. One way to do this is to feed small amounts of food throughout the day, instead of one big meal, allowing the tortoise to completely finish each small meal before providing another one. If this is impractical for you, then be sure to leave your tortoise no more food at once than she can eat during the day, to prevent uneaten food from spoiling. Any uneaten food must be removed at the end of the day to prevent pests and parasites from contaminating it.

Many tortoises, even if they don't hibernate in the winter, will reduce their food intake and become inactive through the cooler months. This will do no

*Your turtle should be able to climb into her water dish if she's in the mood for a soak. Make sure the water is replaced every day.*

# How to Feed Your Tortoise

There are many things to keep in mind when you're feeding a tortoise. The diet of wild tortoises depends on the type of habitat they live in. Tortoises from arid grassland or desert regions, such as Sulcata, Leopard, and Russian tortoises, eat grasses exclusively. Their digestive system functions much like that of a cow—they use bacteria in their intestines to ferment the plant food they consume to extract usable sugars and proteins. Tortoises from wetter forest areas, such as Redfoot, Yellowfoot, and Hingeback tortoises, include some fallen fruits in their diet, and also a small amount of insect and invertebrate prey. Terrestrial turtles from temperate forests, such as Box turtles, eat a variety of plant foods, as well as invertebrates such as earthworms, salamanders, and insects.

These diets are not interchangeable, and feeding an improper diet is one of the leading causes of death among captive tortoises.

The grassland and desert tortoises do well on a diet made up almost entirely of fresh hay (not straw). This is similar to the grasses that are found in their wild habitats. Ordinary lawn clippings can also be added, as long as the lawn is not chemically treated. This hay and grass mixture should make up three-quarters of the diet. The remaining one-fourth can consist of high-fiber plants such as clover, dandelion, and chicory (all common lawn weeds), and flowers such as hibiscus, roses, geraniums, pansies, and nasturtiums.

Fruits should not be fed to tortoises who come from arid habitats. The rich sugars in fruits will cause an explosive increase in bacteria in the

harm, as long as the tortoise has been eating properly throughout the summer and fall, but you should still offer her food throughout the winter.

## Water for Your Tortoise

All turtles, even terrestrial tortoises from hot, dry regions, should have access to clean drinking water at all times. Aquatic turtles drink regularly by swallowing a small amount of water with their food. Terrestrial turtles must have access to a water dish, particularly after they have been fed. Turtles drink by submerging their heads and using pumping motions in the throat to draw in water.

Any bowl shallow enough for the turtle to reach into and heavy enough not to be tipped over is a suitable water bowl. Many terrestrial turtles also like to tortoise's intestines, producing diarrhea and dehydration. Russian, Sulcata, and Leopard tortoises should never be offered any animal proteins as food, either. That means no cheese, eggs, dog or cat food, monkey biscuits, or canned "turtle diet." Excess protein in the diet, coupled with a deficiency of calcium, produces a condition known as pyramiding, where the shell becomes bumpy and deformed. Too much protein can also cause fatal kidney and liver problems.

Tortoises who are native to wetter forest habitats, such as Redfoot, Yellowfoot, and Hingeback tortoises, can handle a richer diet than the arid grassland species. These tortoises can be fed a diet similar to that of iguanas. About half their diet should consist of leafy green vegetables such as collard greens, mustard greens, endive, and dandelions. Iceberg lettuce should be avoided, as it has virtually no nutritive value; cabbage, spinach, and kale should also be avoided, because these vegetables contain chemical oxalates that remove calcium and can cause nutritional deficiencies.

The rest of the diet should consist of fresh fruits and vegetables, including apples, melons, mangoes, kiwi, squash, and zucchini. High-protein veggies such as peas and beans should be avoided, as should high-oxalate plants like broccoli and cauliflower. Bananas contain high levels of phosphorus and should only be offered as an occasional treat.

This diet can be supplemented with edible flowers. About once a week, animal protein can be provided in the form of a spoonful of canned dog food, a few killed crickets, or a frozen and thawed "pinkie" (newborn) mouse.

soak occasionally, so the water dish should be large enough for the turtle to climb inside. Since many terrestrial turtles cannot swim, the water level should be just barely high enough to cover the turtle's legs.

It is important to replace the water daily. Dirty or polluted water makes a perfect breeding ground for salmonella and other disease organisms.

# Aquatic Turtles

Feeding aquatic turtles is entirely different than feeding terrestrial turtles and tortoises. Land turtles require nothing more than a plate of proper food from which they can graze whenever they want. Feeding aquatic turtles is not quite so simple.

In general, aquatic turtles are more carnivorous than their terrestrial cousins. As they get older, Sliders, Painted turtles, and Red-Bellied turtles add more plant material to their diet. The large predatory turtles, such as Snappers and Matamatas, however, are exclusively carnivorous.

Aquatic turtles cannot use their tongue to manipulate food for swallowing, and depend on the rush of water to help push their prey down into their stomach. It is therefore difficult for aquatic turtles to swallow their food unless they are underwater.

## Messy Eaters

As you can imagine, eating is a messy affair for aquatic turtles. Since they have no teeth and cannot chew their food, turtles must tear their prey into bite-size pieces, using their powerful jaws and strong claws. This, of course, scatters a large amount of detritus and waste particles in the tank. These particles settle to the bottom and decay, quickly causing intolerable odor and cleanliness problems. In a large tank with several turtles, even the most powerful of filters will not be able to keep up with the mess.

The solution to this problem is to feed the turtles in a separate container that is large enough to hold just the turtle. Small aquariums make good feeding containers, but in a pinch such things as sweater boxes or large bowls can be pressed

*Feeding your turtles in a separate "dining" box will help keep the mess to a minimum.*

into service. The idea is to place the turtle into the feeding tank, which contains enough water for the turtle to submerge herself, and then introduce the food. The turtle is then able to rip and tear her food and make as much of a mess as she wants, dirtying up the feeding tank rather than her home tank. After the turtle is finished eating, she can be rinsed off with warm water to remove any food particles or detritus, and then returned to her home tank. The feeding tank is emptied, thoroughly cleaned, and is ready for the next mealtime.

Unfortunately, Snappers and Softshells, who tend to be the messiest eaters, should not be handled for feeding. If you keep these species, you will have to use powerful filters and resign yourself to replacing the water in the tank very often.

## Fish as Food

Probably the best food for most aquatic turtles is live goldfish and earthworms. With the viscera and bones, goldfish provide a healthy, staple diet that is usually eagerly accepted. It is best to stun or kill the fish before feeding them to the turtles, since it may take awhile for your turtle to pursue and capture her food if it is alive—and some turtles, such as Musk and Mud turtles, may not be fast enough to catch live fish. (In the wild, Musk and Mud turtles mostly scavenge

*Live goldfish make a healthy meal for an aquatic turtle. This turtle is in a separate feeding box for her meal.*

## Special Hunting Strategies

Alligator Snappers and Matamatas have developed specialized methods of preying on fish. The Matamata, when she senses a potential meal nearby, swells out her neck, creating a vacuum, and then opens her mouth. The resulting rush of water pulls the fish into the turtle's mouth, where it is swallowed.

The Alligator Snapper hunts by resting motionless on the bottom of a pond or river and holding her jaws open, where her camouflage shell makes her virtually invisible. Inside the mouth is a pink outgrowth of the tongue that looks remarkably like a worm, and this continuously twitches and wiggles. When a curious fish approaches to investigate, the snapper's jaws close on it in an instant, pinning her prey.

The common Snapping turtle does not have a lure like the Alligator Snapper, but she also depends on her natural camouflage to rest motionless in the water, snapping up any passing prey with her long, snakelike neck.

on prey that is already dead.) It is best to always feed your aquatic turtles in a separate feeding tank.

Larger turtles will eat correspondingly larger fish, and for convenience these fish can be kept frozen and then thawed just before feeding. It is very important that any frozen food be thoroughly thawed before feeding, because incompletely thawed food can cause severe intestinal problems.

## Commercial Pellets

Another good food is commercial trout pellets, which can sometimes be found in tropical fish stores. Many reptile stores also sell commercial turtle food sticks, which are usually made from fish products. These are also nutritionally complete and do not make as much mess as whole fish.

Commercial turtle foods that consist of dried "ant eggs" (actually the dried pupae) have virtually no nutritional value and should be strictly avoided, as should foods consisting of dried, vitamin-dusted flies.

## Other Treats

Most aquatic turtles will also eat snails (shell and all), and these are nutritious as well as being a good source of calcium. Occasional treats of raw, lean meat, such as heart or liver, can also be offered, but only rarely and never as a staple food.

Adult aquatic turtles will also eat vegetable matter. Small amounts of fresh, leafy greens, such as escarole, endive, dandelion leaf, and kale can be offered to any adult turtle at every other meal.

*Both terrestrial and aquatic turtles do not need a lot of food. Remove anything that is not eaten before it spoils.*

## Feeding Schedules

Like their terrestrial cousins, aquatic turtles can get by on a surprisingly small amount of food if necessary, easily going for two or three weeks without being fed while their keeper is away. Although they should be fed regularly two or three times a week, they can easily tolerate skipping a few meals now and then.

Since aquatic turtles have a high-protein diet that contains lots of meat, they can get by with much smaller amounts of food than their terrestrial cousins. Fifteen to twenty goldfish or earthworms, spread out over the week, is sufficient food for most adult Sliders. Young turtles, and smaller adults such as Musk turtles, will do well on two or three goldfish or worms per meal. These can be supplemented once a week or so with a few trout pellets or small pieces of raw lean meat.

## What About Supplements?

It is necessary to supplement your turtle's diet with vitamins and minerals. Calcium, in combination with proper ultraviolet lighting, is especially important for young turtles, since it is used to produce healthy bones and shells.

Whole fish, bones included, is a good source of calcium, and should form the staple diet of any aquatic turtle. Additional calcium can be provided by placing a small piece of chalk or limestone in the turtle's feeding tank, where it will dissolve and release small amounts of calcium into the water. Whenever the turtle is fed, she will swallow some of the dissolved calcium along with her food.

If you are feeding your turtles in a separate feeding tank, calcium supplements can be provided by lightly dusting the turtle's food with a phosphorus-free calcium powder.

## Chapter 7

# Keeping Your Turtle Healthy

In general, turtles are quite hardy animals, and as long as they are kept in the proper conditions, they are unlikely to ever develop a medical emergency. However, captive turtles are subject to a number of ailments, several of which can be life threatening if they are not promptly identified and treated.

If your turtle is maintained under proper conditions, it is unlikely that he will ever need more than an annual checkup from the vet. However, problems can arise, and you should be able to recognize the onset of a poor health, deal with a minor problem, and determine if your turtle needs to get to the vet.

## Finding a Veterinarian

Finding a good veterinarian for your turtle may be one of your most difficult tasks. While most vets are well trained in small animal care, only a few have had any training in the unique medical requirements of reptiles and amphibians. As a result, most veterinarians will flatly refuse to examine your turtle.

Some who decide to try may have no practical experience whatsoever with reptiles, and very little training beyond a single course or two in herp anatomy and physiology. Keep in mind that unless you live in or near a large urban area, you are unlikely to find a vet who has had any meaningful training in reptile care.

### How to Find the Right Veterinarian

The first choice is to approach your local herpetological society for help. Your local herp society deals with qualified veterinarians all the time, in matters such as adoptions and rescues. Most of the competent reptile vets are likely to be members of the herp society, as well.

Another choice, if you have a local wildlife rehabilitation center or zoo nearby, is to ask for their help. They might be able to point you to a good herp vet. You can also look online—several sites list herp veterinarians by state (see the appendix). The final option is to call any veterinarian in the phone book and ask for a recommendation to a good reptile veterinarian.

> **TIP**
>
> **Choosing a Veterinarian**
>
> Select a vet before bringing your turtle home.
>
> Ask friends for recommendations.
>
> Check with a local herp society.
>
> Ask if the vet is a member of the Association of Reptile and Amphibian Veterinarians.
>
> Feel free to ask questions and seek second opinions.

## The Checkup

Once you have found a suitable vet, it is a good idea to make an appointment for a checkup. This enables you to get to know the vet and your vet to get to know your turtle. The vet will examine your turtle for external parasites and the most common diseases. Your turtle will also probably be weighed and measured.

*An initial veterinary exam when your turtle first comes home will help establish what is normal for your pet, so you and your vet will know when things are not normal.*

# Salmonella

The health concern that comes up most often when discussing turtles, ironically, does not usually affect the turtle at all. Instead, it attacks the turtle's owner.

The incidence of salmonella disease contracted from pet turtles is often exaggerated (many more people get the disease from handling raw chicken than from handling pet turtles). Nevertheless, it is a fact that the salmonella bacteria, which can produce severe gastrointestinal disease, can be found living naturally on the shells and skin of turtles, particularly aquatic turtles.

Under natural conditions, salmonella never builds up to a level where it can produce infections. In captivity, however, particularly when the tank is not kept sufficiently cleaned, the salmonella population can explode and congregate in the water. From there it is transferred to the turtle's shell and skin, and then transferred to your hands.

It is illegal to sell any turtle in the United States who has not been certified to be free of salmonella. To eliminate the bacteria, most turtle breeders treat their tanks with the antibiotic gentamicin. Unfortunately, this has now produced a

*Always wash your hands with soap and water after handling your turtle or anything in his tank or enclosure. This is the easiest way to prevent the spread of salmonella.*

drug-resistant strain of salmonella—a serious matter, since gentamicin is also the drug used to treat human victims of salmonella poisoning.

## Take Precautions

Since it is impossible to kill all the bacteria, it is a safe assumption that any turtle you see will have at least some salmonella organisms living on his shell. What can you do?

Fortunately, a few simple precautions can virtually eliminate the danger of contracting a salmonella infection from a captive turtle. First, always wash your hands after handling any reptile or anything from a reptile's tank or cage. Although washing with plain water is ineffective, washing with soap will kill the salmonella organism.

In an aquatic turtle tank, an efficient filtration system using activated charcoal is absolutely vital to remove waste products, uneaten food, and other pollutants that can encourage the growth of the bacteria. Still, it does not eliminate the necessity of periodically replacing a portion of the water. (If you feed your turtles in a separate container, controlling bacteria in the main tank becomes much easier.)

For a terrestrial turtle, be sure your turtle's cage, tank, or enclosure is kept clean, that feces are removed promptly, and that the water in his water dish is changed often.

### Salmonella Stoppers

Follow these simple rules and you are unlikely to ever have any salmonella problems with your turtles.

- Always wash your hands after handling any turtle.
- Use soap; it kills the salmonella organism.
- Make sure your turtle's water (aquatic or terrestrial) is always clean and change it often to prevent the bacteria from building up.
- Supervise small children when they are near a turtle. Do not let them put the turtle in their mouths, or put their fingers in their mouths after handling the turtle.

Never allow a reptile to come in contact with any surface that is used to prepare your food, such as kitchen counters, sinks, and food dishes, and make sure you wash your own hands before touching any such surfaces yourself.

Always supervise small children when they are near the turtle. Do not let them put their fingers in their mouths while handling the turtle, and make sure they wash their hands promptly afterward.

If these simple rules are followed, it is unlikely that you will ever have any salmonella problems with your reptiles.

# Wounds

Minor wounds and scrapes on a terrestrial turtle can be treated by dabbing on an antibiotic cream, such as Neosporin, onto the injury. Turtles, like most reptiles, have very good internal healing mechanisms, and most minor injuries will heal by themselves in a few weeks.

If the turtle is improperly housed, he can receive minor burns from a heat lamp or a sizzle stone. These can also be treated with antibiotic cream.

Creams such as Neosporin, however, are not of much use with aquatic turtles, since they are quickly washed off. Aquatic turtles who have suffered a minor wound should be soaked in a separate tank containing a liquid solution of antibiotic such as Betadine, which can usually be found at the drugstore. A ten-minute soaking twice a day is sufficient for most minor injuries. The turtle should be rinsed off in clean water before being returned to his normal tank.

# Respiratory Infections

Signs of a respiratory infection are runny eyes, discharge from the nose, gasping or wheezing breaths, and breathing with the mouth open. This problem is nearly always the result of keeping the turtle in conditions that are too cool or drafty. Tortoises from desert or tropical regions can develop colds if they are chilled for even a very short period of time. Untreated, the infection can spread to the lungs and cause a fatal case of pneumonia.

If the infection is not severe, it can usually be cleared up by raising the temperature in the turtle's tank by 5 or 10 degrees for a few days. If the symptoms persist, or if the turtle begins having noticeable difficulty breathing, it's time for a trip to the veterinarian.

*This turtle has a nice clean face. Runny eyes, nasal discharge, wheezing, or breathing with an open mouth are signs of a respiratory infection.*

Most respiratory infections are treated with antibiotic injections. Your vet will give you a supply of needles and show you how to administer the shots. The treatment usually lasts about three weeks.

## Intestinal Infections

There is no mistaking the symptoms of an intestinal infection. The turtle will void smelly, slimy feces, which are watery and loose. Aquatic turtles will quickly turn their tanks into a cesspool, while terrestrial turtles will have you working overtime cleaning their substrate.

There are two possible culprits, and it usually takes a veterinarian to determine the actual cause of infection. One possibility is that protozoans have infected the turtle's intestinal lining. Another is that salmonella bacteria may have built up in the water to such high levels that they have infected the turtle. (This is a sure indication that the tank has not been kept sanitary.) Salmonella is more complicated to treat because it has drug-resistant strains.

# Hibernation

One of the most important factors in any turtle's life is maintaining proper body temperature. In temperate areas, winter daylight hours grow so short and the temperatures drop so low that the turtle is unable to maintain his preferred body temperature. As a result, he is forced to stop eating and retreat to an underground burrow, where his body temperature may drop to as low as 40 degrees Fahrenheit. In other words, he hibernates until warmer temperatures and longer days arrive with the spring.

Hibernation is a stressful and dangerous time for a turtle. A considerable proportion of wild turtles die during their hibernation period, often because they are discovered and dug up by predators as they hibernate.

With pet tortoises, there are two potential dangers to watch out for: First, the turtle must have stored enough fat over the previous autumn to carry him through the winter, since he will not eat at all until the following spring. Many wild turtles are not able to find enough food to store enough fat, and even though their body functions are greatly slowed during hibernation, they still don't have enough energy to make it. This problem can be prevented by making sure your pet receives sufficient food to store up enough fat to last through the winter.

The other danger is that if the turtle is sick or weakened by improper environmental conditions, his body functions may become so low and weak that hibernation becomes too physiologically stressful on the turtle, and he won't survive the stress.

Many species of turtles do not need to hibernate if they are kept at normal temperatures throughout the winter. They will generally remain active and continue to eat, although they may eat less in the winter than they do the rest of the year.

Some turtles, however, such as Russian tortoises and some Painted turtles, seem to be genetically programmed to hibernate regardless of the surrounding temperature, and may become inactive even if they are kept artificially warm. In these circumstances, it becomes very dangerous to maintain normal body temperatures, since the turtle will refuse to eat even though his metabolic rate remains high. This high rate will very likely use up his fat reserves and cause starvation before the turtle will accept food again in the spring. If your turtle refuses to eat at all during the winter and spends most of his time being inactive in his hide box, you will probably have to allow him to hibernate.

Keep in mind that most tortoises and tropical turtles do not hibernate at all in their natural habitat, and must be kept warm year round.

## Preparing for Hibernation

To prepare a terrestrial turtle for hibernation, gradually reduce the temperature in the tank by a few degrees each day until it is about 50 degrees. At this point, the turtle will be torpid and unmoving. Gently place the turtle in a box packed with slightly damp moss or towels and place the box in a basement, porch, or other area that has a steady temperature between 45 and 50 degrees (some turtle keepers have successfully hibernated turtles by placing them in the refrigerator). Leave the turtle there for at least ten weeks.

At the end of the hibernation period, reverse this process by gradually raising the temperature in the tank a few degrees each day until it reaches normal levels. If all goes well, your turtle should be ready to eat again within a few days of reaching the optimum tank temperature. If you are keeping Russian tortoises in an outdoor pen, they can safely hibernate themselves outside, provided you give them several feet of leaf litter and loose dirt to dig into. As long as the tortoises can dig below the frost line, they will be able to survive any normal North American winter.

During the winter you may need to keep an eye out for skunks, dogs, and other predators that may attempt to dig up hibernating turtles.

Aquatic turtles, such as Red-Eared Sliders and Painted turtles, can hibernate right in their tank, if it becomes necessary. Gradually reduce the water temperature to the low 40s. The turtles will sink to the bottom of the aquarium and stay there, unmoving. During hibernation, aquatic turtles are able to extract oxygen from the surrounding water.

At the end of the hibernation period, reverse this process by gradually raising the temperature in the tank a few degrees each day until it reaches normal levels. If all goes well, your turtle should be ready to eat again within a few days of reaching the optimum tank temperature.

If your aquatic turtle lives in an outdoor year-round pen pond, he will take care of hibernating himself right in the water.

Whatever the cause, intestinal troubles can quickly kill a turtle. If you ever see signs of intestinal problems in your turtle, get him to a vet immediately for a culture and proper treatment.

# Parasites

Parasites, both internal and external, are not usually found in captive-bred turtles, but are fairly common in wild-caught turtles (particularly imported animals). Because aquatic turtles live in water and most of their food consists of aquatic prey such as fish, worms, and snails, they are more susceptible to getting parasites.

## Leeches

The most common external parasites are leeches. They resemble small, dark worms, and attach to the skin at the turtle's neck or legs. They live by sucking blood from their host, and although they are hardly ever found on terrestrial turtles, they are common on wild-caught aquatic animals.

The best treatment is to carefully remove the leech with a pair of tweezers and then wipe the area with a disinfectant or antibiotic cream. Aquatic turtles must be kept out of the water for a day or two to allow the antibiotics to work without being washed off.

## Liver Flukes

A number of internal parasites can infest turtles. The most common are liver flukes, which are found in snails and are passed on to the turtle when he eats the snail.

Nearly any wild-caught aquatic turtle you get will be infested with flukes. Usually, they do no great harm, but very heavy infestations can destroy the internal organs and kill your turtle. The symptoms are loss of appetite and rapid weight loss. Severe infestations must be treated by a veterinarian.

## Intestinal Worms

If your turtle seems to be eating a lot but not gaining weight, he may have intestinal worms such as nematodes. Nearly all wild turtles are regularly exposed to these parasites, and all wild-caught animals will probably be infected.

Nematodes, like most internal parasites that attack turtles, have complex life cycles, parts of which are spent inside snails, fish, or worms. Usually, the eggs are passed in turtle feces and ingested by snails, where they hatch. The young nematodes are then swallowed by the turtle when he eats the snail, entering the digestive tract to begin the process again.

Even if your turtle is captive-born and has never been exposed to the wild, he may contract parasites by eating contaminated food. For this reason, both wild-caught and captive-bred turtles must be examined regularly for worms and other parasites. You may see worms in the turtle's feces—they look like tiny bits of thread. The worms can weaken the turtle by robbing him of nutrients. Heavy infestations can damage the intestines or other internal organs.

*Parasites spend part of their lifecycle in other animals, such as worms. So even a captive-bred turtle may end up with intestinal parasites after eating an infected animal.*

If you suspect that your turtle has worms, you must take a recent fecal sample to your vet and have it examined. Intestinal worms can be treated with a dewormer, which is usually slipped to the reptile in his food or given as oral drops.

## Cloacal Prolapse

Prolapses occur when the lining of the cloaca protrudes from the anal opening and is exposed outside the body. In some cases, part of the small intestine may also be exposed, and in female turtles the ovaries may also be extended. The cause of cloacal prolapse is not known; it may be a combination of several factors, including stress or the presence of intestinal worms.

Although prolapses are horrifying to look at, they are not usually life-threatening to the turtle. Still, they require immediate treatment. If your turtle suffers a prolapse, it is very important to keep the protruding organs moist. With an aquatic turtle, of course, this presents no problem; terrestrial turtles, however, should be placed in a bowl of shallow water to keep the organs damp. If the prolapsed tissues dry out, they will die, and a veterinarian will then have to remove the dead tissues surgically.

Usually, if you can entice the turtle to move around a bit, the prolapse will work itself back in. If necessary, you can gently massage the areas surrounding the protrusion, but you should never attempt to push or force the organs back in. Most often, the prolapse will correct itself after a few days. If it doesn't, it's time to see the vet.

It is also important to watch that the turtle does not interfere with the prolapse by clawing at it. The turtle is unable to recognize that the prolapse is a part of his own organs, and may make an effort to detach the "foreign object" from his tail. In addition, other turtles in the tank may attack the prolapse. If a turtle is able to reach the tissue, he can turn it into a bloody mess in a short time. If that happens, surgery will probably be necessary. If you see this happening, gently restrain your turtle and take him to the veterinarian.

Although cloacal prolapses are not all that common, some individual turtles seem to be prone to them and may experience prolapses several times within a short period. In this case, your vet may stitch the cloacal opening to make it tighter and prevent further recurrence.

## Visceral Gout

This is a nutritional disease that is usually found in tortoises rather than aquatic turtles, and is caused by a diet that is too high in fat and protein. Like most reptiles, tortoises are vegetarians and cannot digest animal fat very efficiently, and a steady diet of fatty food can cause uric acid crystals to build up in the kidneys and other internal organs. This causes these organs to literally become rock hard and to stop functioning, which can cause very sudden death.

The disease can be prevented by feeding your turtle a proper diet. Herbivorous tortoises from arid grasslands and deserts, such as Leopard, Russian, and Sulcata tortoises, cannot digest animal proteins of any sort and should not be fed any animal-based foods. Omnivorous Redfoot and Hingeback tortoises can be fed lean meats, such as fish- or chicken-based dog foods, but only in very small amounts.

# Skin and Shell Problems

## Algae

After a time, your aquatic turtle may begin to sport a rather unattractive coating of green slime, which may also begin to cover the inside of the tank and other exposed surfaces. Occasionally, it may become so thick that the water itself will turn bright green, making it impossible to see anything inside the tank. This is algae, and it is completely harmless to the turtle (although it will probably drive you nuts). In the slower-moving aquatic turtles, such as Matamatas, a thick, heavy coat of algae serves as camouflage for their ambush style of hunting.

Do not treat a buildup of algae in the tank with chemical algaecides, because most of these contain hydrochloric acid, which can be harmful to the turtles. You can help reduce algae growth by keeping the tank light on for a shorter period.

Some hobbyists keep a number of large snails or algae-eating fish in the turtle tank for the express purpose of grazing all the algae, but the presence of these animals will complicate the task of keeping the tank clean, since they contribute additional waste products. The best way to prevent algae buildup is to periodically change a portion of the tank water—which you should be doing anyway.

*Your aquatic turtle may end up with algae on his shell. Keeping the water clean will help prevent this.*

## Fungus

If, instead of slimy green splotches you begin to see cottony white tufts on the turtle's shell or skin, it's time to worry. This is fungus, and it usually attacks the turtle at a site where the skin or scutes have been injured.

Since most turtles prefer the warm, damp conditions that favor fungal growth, fungal spores are always present and waiting for an opportunity to invade. If the fungus gets underneath the scutes, it can penetrate the carapace or plastron and produce large, gaping holes, a condition known as ulcerative shell disease. Eventually, the fungus will enter the body cavity, which will be fatal to the turtle.

Fortunately, fungal infections are easily treated. The best remedy is to place the infected turtle in a weak solution of iodine (just enough iodine to color the water) for a ten-minute soak, twice a day. Between treatments, keep the turtle dry (aquatic turtles will need to be kept in a dry land area and prohibited from entering the water) and maintain a slightly higher temperature in the environment.

To help prevent fungal infection, make sure your turtle always has a warm, dry area in the tank for basking, where he can dry off completely. Even in aquatic tanks, the land area must be bone dry. Perpetually damp conditions can lead to fungal infections.

# Beaks and Claws

Unlike snakes and lizards, which shed their skin in large flakes or all in one piece, turtles replace their skin gradually by continuously flaking off tiny pieces. Therefore, turtles are not prone to the shedding problems that can affect other reptiles. However, captive turtles are prone to one problem that lizards and snakes never face. The turtle's horny jaw sheaths grow continuously throughout his life, as do his claws—much like human fingernails.

Captive turtles are not always able to wear down their beaks and claws quickly enough. So for the turtle to walk and chew properly, it may sometimes be necessary to have a veterinarian trim your pet's beak and claws.

The problem can be prevented by allowing your tortoise to roam outdoors and graze on plants, where the rough surfaces will wear down the tortoise's claws and beak. This is usually only a problem with Box turtles, who are often given diets of soft mushy foods that don't wear down their beaks. Tortoises eat a lot of grasses, and the silica particles in grasses wear down the beaks.

*urtles living the easy life in your home may not wear down their beaks and claws naturally. Your terinarian can check them and trim both, if necessary.*

# ¯he Calcium Balancing Act

ɔung aquatic turtles are particularly susceptible to calcium deficiencies, mani-sted by soft, rubbery shells and malformed limbs. This is nearly always the sult of an improper diet, but can also be caused by insufficient vitamin D3 due ɔ a lack of exposure to UV-B wavelengths.

Treatment consists of calcium supplements and increased ultraviolet light, ut if the condition persists, it can lead to permanent deformities or even death. he best prevention is a proper diet, with calcium supplements and calcium-ch foods, such as whole fish or, for herbivorous tortoises, grasses and hay. The isease can also be avoided by providing adequate access to unfiltered natural unlight or, failing that, to an artificial UV-B lamp.

Shell problems in tortoises can also occur when there is too much protein in ie diet and not enough calcium. The protein causes rapid growth, but the lack f calcium means the shell cannot expand rapidly enough to keep up. The first gn of this is called *pyramiding*, in which the carapace is covered by triangular imps where the scutes are growing improperly. If untreated, the deficiency can roduce severe shell deformations. Pyramiding can be prevented by a proper iet and access to calcium supplements and UV light.

# Part III

# Turtles in Our World

## Chapter 8

# Your Turtle's Behavior

One of the reasons we choose to live with animals is to experience other creatures and different ways of looking at the world. Turtles are certainly *very* different from us! Sometimes, if they are basking on a piece of wood or chewing very slowly on a green leaf, it may seem as if they are just slow, decorative creatures. But, like all animals, turtles have priorities and preferences, and ways of communicating with the creatures around them.

The more you learn about your turtle's behavior, the more interesting she will be. She's far more than just a pretty shell!

## How Smart Are Turtles?

The structure of a turtle's brain is somewhat similar to that of a bird, but the turtle, like all reptiles, lacks the greatly enlarged cerebral hemispheres found in birds and mammals. Since these are the areas of the brain that control learning and reasoning, most turtles don't share the intelligence of warm-blooded creatures.

Some turtles are no intellectual slouches, though. In some species, the brain reaches a size relative to body weight that is comparable to some birds, and these turtles, while unable to approach the brainier mammals, nevertheless seem to have mental faculties that function at a much higher level than was previously suspected.

The most intelligent turtle is reputed to be the North American Wood turtle (*Glyptemis insculpta*), who has been the subject of laboratory tests and experiments. In controlled experiments using food rewards, Wood turtles can learn to

*Aquatic turtles, such as these Red-Eared Sliders, don't mind being on top of or on the edge of things.*

run a maze almost as quickly as laboratory rats. They can also retain what they have learned for several weeks, and can successfully recall mazes they had not been exposed to for some time.

## Spatial Sense

One series of experiments has studied the spatial sense of various turtles. In these experiments, a deep hole in the floor was covered over with a clear sheet of glass and various types of animals were released at the edge of the "cliff." Less intelligent animals, such as certain lizards, did not hesitate when they reached the cliff edge, and ran right across the glass—presumably, had it been a real cliff, they would have unthinkingly plunged to their doom. Visually oriented mammals, such as rats, approached the edge of the simulated cliff with caution and refused to step beyond it onto the glass.

Interestingly, aquatic turtles such as Painted turtles took no notice of the cliff, and scrambled at top speed right across the glass. Terrestrial turtles, however, such as Box turtles, did not venture beyond the edge. The explanation for this behavior seems to be that aquatic turtles are accustomed to basking over water, where they can safely dive from a height to escape predators. Thus they have no need for highly refined spatial abilities.

## Learning Ability

In captivity, many turtles display the ability to learn. Aquatic turtles who are fed at the same time every day soon learn when it is feeding time and will be ready and waiting when their keeper approaches. Tame turtles will also be able to distinguish their keeper from other people, and will often swim to just that person to be fed. Terrestrial tortoises learn even more quickly who their keeper is, and often display an inclination to follow them around.

The more intelligent turtles can learn to respond to their names, making them a sort of reptilian prodigy. Thus, while your turtle will never learn to do tricks or to fetch the newspaper, she may be able to at least recognize who you are and respond to you.

# Handling Your Turtle

Since few people are afraid of turtles, it is much more likely that you will want to handle your pet turtle than you would a snake or lizard. Unfortunately, most turtles, particularly the aquatic species, do not take well to handling and are not very responsive to physical contact with their owners.

Although some aquatic turtles do become tame and some may even learn to take food from their owner's fingers, most will make a hasty retreat to the bottom of the tank if you approach and try to pick them up. Aquatic turtles do not like being held or handled, and tend not to be very playful or sociable pets.

Terrestrial turtles, on the other hand, seem to be much more intelligent than their aquatic counterparts, and often become very responsive toward their keepers. Many a tortoise will follow you around like a puppy, often clawing at your shoes, begging you to rub her head or scratch her shell—or more often, give her a tidbit of whatever you are eating.

For the most part, however, all turtles should be carried around as little as possible. Although tortoises and terrestrial turtles sometimes enjoy having their head or neck rubbed or their shell patted, they also prefer to keep all four legs firmly on the ground.

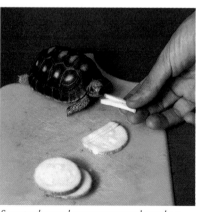

*Some turtles may become tame enough to take a snack from your fingers.*

# Holding Your Turtle

Of course, it may sometimes be necessary to pick up a turtle, either for health-care reasons or to carry out necessary cage-cleaning or maintenance tasks. Even though turtles are well protected in their shells, they are susceptible to injury if they are not properly handled. Some turtles are capable of injuring you if they are handled incorrectly.

> **TIP**
>
> If you are keeping a Snapping turtle, you can pretty much forget ever holding your turtle (unless you want your nickname to be Three-Fingered Louie). These turtles think nothing at all of biting the hand that feeds them.

The best way to hold most turtles is to grasp the shell gently but firmly at the sides with your fingers, at the same time allowing the turtle's feet to rest in the open palm of your other hand. If the turtle gets excited, she will make kicking or swimming motions with her feet and legs, but she will not escape as long as you are gripping her shell.

With larger turtles, you will need to use both hands—one on each side of the shell—extending your fingers underneath the plastron to support the turtle's weight. This will leave the feet dangling, however, which the turtle may not

*Pick up your turtle by grasping her firmly on either side of her shell. As soon as you lift her, slide your other hand underneath so her feet rest on your open palm.*

> **Characteristics of Your Turtle**
>
> Long-lived
>
> Independent
>
> Inquisitive
>
> Adaptable
>
> Hearty appetite

particularly like. When holding any turtle, watch out for her feet; turtles have sharp claws and may scratch you if they begin flailing their limbs in an effort to get down.

Long-necked turtles, such as Softshells, will be able to reach back along their shell and bite you. The safest way to carry these turtles is to grasp the rear legs (not the tail) and use them as handles. Keep the plastron side of the turtle's body facing toward you, and hold the turtle as far from your legs as possible.

Be very careful that you do not drop your turtle! Wet aquatic turtles can be very slippery and difficult to hold, and even terrestrial tortoises can kick and wriggle their way free. Falls can result in cracked shells or internal organ damage that can be fatal.

## Transporting a Turtle

Sometimes it's necessary to transport a turtle, either for a visit to the vet or to use in a talk or educational show.

Very small turtles, whether terrestrial or aquatic, can be transported in a snake bag. This is simply a large cloth bag, about 18 inches long and a foot or so wide (a pillowcase makes a good improvised snake bag). Place the little turtle into the bag, along with a handful of damp paper towels. Tightly twist the top portion of the bag and tie it in a loose overhand knot so you can conveniently carry it around. Since the weave of most cloth bags is not airtight, the turtle will be able to breathe right through the bag. Be careful that nobody steps or sits on the bag.

Larger turtles usually can't be bagged, since their sharp claws can make quick work of the cloth and they will easily shred their way to freedom. They can be safely transported in a box; punch a number of air holes in the sides, put in the turtle, then securely tape the top closed. The box should also contain wads of newspaper or clean cloths to prevent the turtle from being bounced around too much during the trip. Make sure the air temperature in the car is warm enough for the turtle. If you are transporting a large Snapper or Softshell turtle, it is best to use a wooden box rather than cardboard.

*It may be tough to take a large tortoise anywhere.*

Keep in mind that an adult tortoise of the larger species, such as a Sulcata or Leopard tortoise, can weigh more than 75 pounds. Transporting these beasts is a task that may well prove to be virtually impossible.

## Kids and Turtles

Turtles and tortoises can make good pets for children, provided you keep a few basic points in mind:

- Turtles are not cuddly or responsive pets. Reptiles cannot develop the emotional bonds to their keeper that a dog or cat will.
- Most turtles and tortoises do not enjoy being picked up or played with.
- Turtles require constant care. Every day, your child will need to perform such tasks as feeding, cage cleaning, and changing the water. If your child cannot perform these tasks responsibly, it will fall upon you to do them.

- Turtles require a lot of equipment. You will need, at minimum, a large tank or enclosure, a basking lamp, and an ultraviolet lamp. For aquatic turtles, you will also need a powerful filtration system.
- Turtles can spread disease to children who do not follow the basic safety steps. Children who kiss their turtles, or who neglect to wash their hands after handling a turtle, are at risk for salmonella.

For children who are responsible enough to provide proper care and take proper safety precautions, however, turtles can make interesting, long-lived pets and may spark a lifelong interest in the natural world and the diversity of life all around us.

### Curious Kids

You can teach them:

- How to hold a turtle
- Things to feed a turtle
- Not to kiss a turtle
- Ways to give a turtle a safe home
- About different types of turtles

# Chapter 9

# Chelonian Conservation

**I**n the United States today, more than a dozen turtle species are listed by the federal government as threatened or endangered, and several dozen more have become threatened in various states. Worldwide, many turtles, including every single member of the large and varied family of sea turtles, are considered threatened or endangered in the wild and are vulnerable to extinction.

Unfortunately, and to our everlasting shame, nearly all of these species have become endangered through the actions of humans. These actions range from the unintentional but foreseeable (such as draining, cutting down, and developing the habitats upon which turtles depend), to the deliberate and malicious (such as harvesting sea turtles, which pointlessly kills large numbers every year).

For the most part, the major conservation groups have not demonstrated any particular interest in endangered or threatened reptiles. (One notable exception has been increased efforts to protect endangered sea turtles.) Fortunately, though, there are people fighting to preserve our turtle and reptile biodiversity, along with the rest of our endangered ecosystems. And, since the pet trade has traditionally been a primary offender in driving many species to the brink of extinction, it seems only fitting that today's responsible pet owners and turtle keepers have important roles to play in herp conservation. Therefore, I will end this book with information on what you, as a responsible turtle keeper, can do to help to preserve and protect these unique animals.

*Sea turtles are among the few reptile species that have been the subject of intensive conservation efforts.*

# Herpetological Societies

The bulk of all herpetological education and conservation work in the United States is done, either directly or indirectly, by national, state, and local herpetological societies. These are nonprofit bodies formed by groups of private citizens to further public education about reptiles and amphibians and promote the conservation of wild herps. Herpetological societies also promote responsible keeping and captive breeding of turtles and other reptiles and amphibians.

I cannot encourage you strongly enough to join your local herpetological society. Membership in a herpetological society can cost between $15 and $35 per year, and it is an investment that is well worth making for any turtle enthusiast. Not only do you gain access to a rich source of experience and advice, but you will be helping to play an important role in maintaining and protecting these fascinating creatures.

**What You Can Do**

Educate children to respect endangered animals.

Keep your turtle free of salmonella.

Share your resources with new turtle owners.

Make a commitment to be a responsible turtle keeper.

## Research Assistance

To help them meet their goals, herpetological societies carry out a number of tasks. Many do annual field surveys in which volunteer teams comb wildlife habitats to take a census of the local reptile and amphibian populations. This enables researchers to study population trends of various species and provides advance warning if populations of certain species are beginning to decline. It also helps state and federal officials monitor the populations of animals listed as threatened or endangered.

## Conservation Efforts

Most herp societies also work with national conservation groups, such as the Nature Conservancy. These groups raise money to purchase reptile and amphibian habitats, to maintain them in a natural state, and to ensure that they will not be destroyed by future development. A few of the larger herp societies may even own and maintain reptile preserves.

Special mention should be made here of the Mid-Atlantic Reptile Show, held annually in Baltimore, Maryland. All of the proceeds from this show go directly toward purchasing habitat areas in Costa Rica for turtles and other wildlife, and some eight hundred acres of rain forest have already been secured.

## Public Education

The most visible work of herpetological societies is in the area of public education. Most herp societies sponsor talks and shows for the public where reptiles and amphibians are exhibited and people can learn about the vital roles that reptiles play in various ecosystems.

Speakers are usually made available for school classrooms, Boy Scout and Girl Scout troops, and other groups or organizations that are interested in reptile and wildlife conservation. State and local herpetological societies may also provide witnesses and information for lawmakers who are considering regulations that would affect reptiles and their keepers.

Herpetological societies also work hard to ensure that all reptiles kept in captivity are kept safely, responsibly, and in a way that does not endanger any wild populations. Through newsletters, meetings, guest lectures, and other methods, herp societies disseminate a large amount of information and advice about the captive care and breeding of a wide variety of turtles and other reptiles and amphibians.

*These giant Aladabra tortoises help visitors to the Knoxville Zoo understand how fascinating turtles can be.*

## Pet Welfare

Herp society members monitor local pet shops, ensuring that any reptiles and amphibians offered for sale are being kept in adequate conditions.

Many local herp societies also work closely with local veterinarians and run adoption services that provide good homes to herps who have been abandoned, confiscated, or seized by local law enforcement or humane society officials, or simply given up for adoption.

# Captive Breeding

One of the most concrete contributions turtle keepers can make to reptile conservation is a vigorous and steady program of captive breeding.

There are two different but important possible goals for a captive-breeding program. The first is breeding endangered and threatened reptiles for the ultimate purpose of reintroducing them into the wild. The major difficulty faced by such programs, of course, is the continuing destruction of habitats, which too often means that there is no longer any "wild" left for the animals to be released into.

Only a few turtles have been the object of intensive captive-breeding attempts. The seven species of sea turtles (all of which are threatened or endangered) have been the target of a program that enables volunteers to monitor

## Spread the Word

If there are no local herpetological societies in your area, do not despair. Your area still contains at least one resource who can help educate the public about the ecological roles played by reptiles and the importance of protecting them. That resource is you.

Probably the most important factor in protecting and preserving reptiles (including turtles) is public education. Although few people have the irrational fear of turtles that they have of snakes or spiders, most people have, at best, only a vague understanding of these animals and their needs, and most of what they do "know" is usually inaccurate.

Public education is probably the most important work that any turtle hobbyist can do. If you are comfortable with public speaking, use your skills to talk to as many people as you can. Go to grade school classrooms, Bible school classes, Boy Scout and Girl Scout troops, or local environmental associations.

If you don't know the scientific names of your pets, or can't identify all of the turtles that are native to Latin America, or can't tell a quadrate bone from a tibia, that's okay. As long as you have an understanding of what ecosystems are and how they work, and what roles turtles play in them (and I hope this book has helped you in that understanding), you know all the important stuff. Beyond that, it is merely a matter of exposing people to the animals, allowing them to see for themselves the unique behavior patterns and the dazzling array of colors that make turtles so fascinating. The animals themselves are their own best advertisement.

known breeding areas and remove the eggs shortly after they are laid. The eggs are then artificially incubated and hatched, and the young turtles released into the wild.

*Captive-breeding programs make turtles available for the pet trade without taking wild turtles out of their natural habitat.*

On the Galapagos Islands, the Darwin Memorial Research Station has been breeding those islands' giant tortoises. Four of the Galapagos subspecies, however, are already extinct, and two others are effectively extinct, since they consist only of very old individuals who are past breeding age.

The second goal of captive breeding is very much within the scope of the amateur breeder and local herpetological societies. One of the chief threats facing many wild populations of turtles, both within the United States and abroad, is overcollection for the pet trade. Few wild populations can withstand that sort of drain for very long.

One partial solution to this problem is to encourage captive breeding of these species, so they can be made available to hobbyists and collectors without the necessity of taking any more animals from the wild. Unfortunately, turtles are not as widely bred as are the more popular lizards or snakes, and captive-bred turtles are a rarity in the pet trade. For this reason, responsible captive breeding of these species should be actively encouraged and supported.

Of course, many of the most endangered species are difficult to breed because we simply do not know enough about their biology and habits to duplicate them in captivity. It therefore becomes a priority for serious hobbyists to identify the conditions under which these turtles can be kept and persuaded to breed. Such knowledge will be vital to protecting and maintaining these species—and serious amateurs are fully capable of discovering and providing such knowledge.

For that reason, I strongly encourage every turtle keeper and hobbyist who has been inspired by this book to gain a level of experience and confidence that will enable you to undertake your own captive-breeding research. Start with those species that breed fairly easily but are not commonly bred—Box turtles and Painted turtles would be good choices. From there, go on to the more difficult and rare species. For many turtles, effective breeding in captivity may be all that stands between the species and extinction.

*Several species of Galapagos Island tortoises are already extinct, but the rest are the subject of careful breeding programs. This is a young Galapagos tortoise.*

# Legal Protections

Until about forty years ago, there were virtually no laws regulating the capture or sale of wild animals. Individuals or businesses were free, within the limits of "animal cruelty" laws, to capture, export or import, and sell any species they wanted to. The unfortunate result was the decimation of many species of wildlife, including reptiles, and the hunting of other species to near extinction.

In the 1960s and early 1970s the growing environmental movement made most people aware of the tremendous damage that humans were doing to our world ecosystems. In this period, a number of laws were passed to protect threatened or endangered species and to regulate the sale and possession of many types of native wildlife.

Most of these laws are still in effect, and may have an impact on the amateur turtle keeper or hobbyist. Because there are so many different state and local laws, this book cannot serve as a guide to the legalities of turtle-keeping. The best I can do is provide a broad overview—it is the responsibility of the individual turtle keeper to know and obey all applicable laws.

## International Laws

Without question, the single most important international agreement affecting reptile keepers and hobbyists is the Convention on the International Trade in Endangered Species (CITES), also known as the Washington Treaty, signed in 1973 and ratified by the United States in 1975. More than 120 nations have joined in signing.

Under CITES, protected animals are divided into two groups. Animals listed under Appendix I of CITES are those in immediate danger of extinction. It is illegal to import or export any of these animals, except for zoos under special permit.

Animals listed under Appendix II are not yet in imminent danger of extinction, but are declining rapidly and must be protected. It is illegal to import or export any of these species unless they were captured under a special permit or unless they were captive-bred.

The primary purpose of CITES is to prevent international smuggling of endangered and threatened animals taken from the wild. Wildlife smuggling is a serious problem; according to some Interpol estimates, the illegal wildlife trade is a $6 billion a year business, placing it just behind illegal drug trafficking and just ahead of illegal arms smuggling.

*Habitat destruction is a huge threat to all animals. This Striped Mud turtle is digging a nest hole in Florida. If she cannot find a suitable place to lay her eggs, she will not be able to reproduce.*

## Capturing Turtles

It is easy to forget that wild animals, after being free in their natural habitat, do not appreciate captivity. Remember that it is illegal and prosecutable under state and federal laws to remove such animals. Think about the kind of unhappy pet this type of turtle would make and the risk you are taking if you capture one. Is it worth it?

## U.S. Federal Laws

The most important of the federal laws pertaining to the collection and raising of turtles and other reptiles is the Endangered Species Act, passed in 1973, shortly after CITES was signed.

### Endangered Species Act

The stated purpose of the Endangered Species Act (ESA) is:

1. To provide a means whereby the ecosystems upon which endangered species depend may be conserved.
2. To provide a program for the conservation of such endangered and threatened species.

Under the ESA, animals (and plants) that are vulnerable to extinction are listed in two categories. The most seriously vulnerable are listed as "endangered species," defined as "any species which is in danger of extinction throughout all or a significant portion of its range." It is illegal to disturb, collect, possess, or sell any of these species.

Organisms not yet endangered but in jeopardy of becoming so in the near future are classified as "threatened," which is defined as "any species which is likely to become an endangered species within the foreseeable future throughout all of a significant portion of its range." Threatened species may be collected, captive-bred, and sold, but only under strict permits that specify legal limits on such collection. Anyone in possession of a threatened species should be able to show that the animal was obtained legally.

## Help Protect Turtles

Start with abiding by conservation legislation—hobbyists and collectors should absolutely refuse to buy any imported wild-caught reptiles, and should not purchase any turtle who was not captive-bred in the United States. You can also check out herp groups in your community and get involved in local efforts; small actions can produce big results!

If you capture your own turtles in the wild or purchase a turtle that is listed as "threatened" or "endangered" from a breeder, the ESA is likely to apply. Responsible turtle keepers should refrain from collecting wild turtles at all (responsible herpers prefer to leave them in the wild where they belong), and instead, buy captive-bred turtles. If you purchase a species that is listed under the ESA, ask for the appropriate documentation to show that your turtle was obtained legally. Any legitimate breeder of endangered or threatened species will be able to do this.

### Sales and Possession Restrictions

There are also federal laws that apply specifically to the sale and possession of turtles. During the 1960s, when baby Red-Eared Sliders were being sold by the hundreds of thousands (and kept in what, for the most part, were appalling and quickly lethal conditions), several states raised concerns about the transfer of salmonella from turtles to children. A few states passed laws making it illegal to sell any turtle at all; several others passed restrictions on the size of turtle that could be sold.

In 1975, the federal government, after concluding that almost a quarter million cases of salmonellosis a year were caused by improperly kept turtles, stepped in and banned the sale of any turtle with a carapace under 4 inches in length (an exception was made for baby turtles to be used for "research and education purposes"). Turtles over 4 inches long, it was assumed, would cost more to buy and thus create a greater incentive for owners to keep and maintain in sanitary conditions, thereby helping to control the salmonella problem.

Today, the information on how to avoid the unsanitary conditions that lead to salmonellosis is widely available and the number of disease cases that can be traced to captive reptiles is extremely low. Nevertheless, the federal restrictions still apply.

## State Laws

State laws affecting reptile keepers fall into two distinct categories: laws that regulate and control the capture and sale of native species, and laws that regulate or limit the types and number of turtles kept within the borders of that state.

For the most part, laws pertaining to the collection of native turtles are enforced by state game or wildlife commissions. In most instances, the various states follow a classification system similar to that of the federal Endangered Species Act. Animals in imminent danger of extinction within the state are classified as "endangered species," while animals that are severely declining in population and could be in danger shortly are listed as "threatened species." In most states, the collection, sale, or possession of any endangered species is illegal. The collection and sale of any threatened species is illegal without a permit, and possession of any threatened species is illegal unless the animal was obtained legally.

It is entirely possible that any particular species can be listed as endangered in one state and only listed as threatened or perhaps not even listed at all in another. The Ornate Box turtle, for example, is a common and widespread species who often appears on dealer lists. In Arkansas, however, this turtle is listed as threatened and is legally protected.

It would be impossible to list all of the various state laws regulating the possession and capture of turtles. Investigate the specific regulations that your state has for keeping turtles.

*These Gopher tortoises are threatened with extinction and are protected by federal and state laws.*

# Learning More About Your Turtle

## Some Good Books

Dodd, Kenneth C., *North American Box Turtles: A Natural History*, University of Oklahoma Press, 2002.

Ernst, Carl, *Turtles of the United States and Canada*, Smithsonian Books, 2000.

Ferri, Vincenzio, *Turtles and Tortoises*, Firefly Books, 2002.

Gibbons, Whitfield J. and George Zug, *Life History and Ecology of the Slider Turtle*, Smithsonian Books, 1993.

Gurley, Russ, *Keeping and Breeding Freshwater Turtles*, Living Art Publishers, 2003.

Orenstein, Ronald, *Turtles, Tortoises and Terrapins: Survivors in Armor*, Firefly Books, 2001.

Palika, Liz, *Turtles and Tortoises For Dummies*, Wiley Publishing, 2001.

Pirog, E.J. *Russian Tortoises*, TFH Publications, 2006.

## Magazines

*Reptiles Magazine*
P.O. Box 6040
Mission Viejo, CA 92690
(800) 876-9112
www.reptilesmagazine.com

# Herpetological Societies and Associations

## National Groups

**American Society of Icthyologists and Herpetologists**
Maureen Donnelly, Florida International University, Biological Sciences
11200 Southwest 8th St.
Miami, FL 33199
www.asih.org

**Society for the Study of Reptiles and Amphibians**
P.O. Box 58157
Salt Lake City, UT 84158
(801) 562-2660
www.ssarherps.org

## Local Groups

This list is far from complete. The societies listed below may be able to direct you to a local herp society that is closer to you.

**Arizona Herpetological Association**
P.O. Box 64531
Phoenix, AZ 85082-4531
(480) 894-1625
www.azreptiles.com

**Tucson Herpetological Society**
P.O. Box 709
Tucson, AZ 85702-0709
tucsonherpsociety.org

**National Turtle & Tortoise Society**
P.O. Box 66935
Phoenix, AZ 85082-6935
(602) ASK-NTTS
www.ntts-az.org

**Arkansas Herpetological Society**
c/o Floyd Perk
Route 2, Box 16
Hensley, AR 72065
(501) 960-4969
www.snakesofarkansas.com

**The Bay Area Amphibian and Reptile Society**
Palo Alto Junior Museum
1451 Middlefield Rd.
Palo Alto, CA 94301
(408) 450-0759
www.baars.org

**California Turtle and Tortoise Club**
Has local chapters all over California.
www.tortoise.org

**San Diego Herpetological Society**
P.O. Box 4036
San Diego, CA 92164-4036
www.kingsnake.com/sdhs/

**Southwestern Herpetologists Society**
P.O. Box 7469
Van Nuys, CA 91409
(818) 503-2052
www.swhs.org

**Desert Tortoise Preserve Committee, Inc.**
4067 Mission Inn Ave.
Riverside, CA 92501
(951) 683-3872
www.tortoise-tracks.org

**Colorado Herpetological Society**
P.O. Box 150381
Lakewood, CO 80215-0381
www.coloherp.org

**The Connecticut Herpetologist's League**
CT State Agriculture Research Station
123 Huntington St.
New Haven, CT 06511
www.kingsnake.com/chl

**Delaware Herp Society**
Ashland Nature Center
Brackenville & Barley Mill Rd.
Hockessin, DE 19707

**Calusa Herpetological Society**
P.O. Box 222
Estero, FL 33928
www.calusaherp.org

**Central Florida Herpetological Society**
P.O. Box 3277
Winter Haven, FL 33885
cflhs.tripod.com

**Jacksonville Herpetological Society**
P.O. Box 57954
Jacksonville, FL 32241
jaxherp.tripod.com

**Suncoast Herpetological Society**
P.O. Box 2725
Dunedin, FL 34697
(727) 942-6700
www.kingsnake.com/suncoast
herpsociety/SHSHome.htm

**Chicago Herpetological Society**
2430 North Cannon Dr.
Chicago, IL 60614
(312) 409-4456
www.chicagoherp.org

**Hoosier Herpetological Society**
P.O. Box 40544
Indianapolis, IN 46240-0544
www.hoosierherpsociety.org

**Kansas Herpetological Society**
5438 Southwest 12th Terrace, Apt. 4
Topeka, KS 66604
www.ku.edu/~khs/

**Kentucky Herpetological Society**
Kathy Hicks
309 New England Court
Louisville, KY 40214
www.kyherpsoc.org

**Louisiana Gulf Coast Herpetological Society**
P.O. Box 113483
Metairie, LA 70011-3483
www.lgchs.org

**Maine Herpetological Society**
99 Water St.
Millinocket, ME 04462
www.kingsnake.com/maineherp

**New England Herpetological Society**
P.O. Box 81
Somerville, MA 02143
(617) 789-5800
www.neherp.com

**Mid-Atlantic Turtle and Tortoise Society**
P.O. Box 22321
Baltimore, MD 21203-4321
www.matts-turtles.org

**Michigan Society of Herpetologists**
321 West Oakland Ave.
Lansing, MI 48906
www.michherp.org

**Minnesota Herpetological Society**
Bell Museum of Natural History
10 Church St., Southeast
Minneapolis, MN 55455-0104
www.bellmuseum.org/herpetology/main.html

**Kansas City Herpetological Society**
P.O. Box 118
Liberty, MO 64069
www.kcherp.com

**St. Louis Herpetological Society**
P.O. Box 410346
St. Louis, MO 63141-0346
www.stlherpsociety.org

**North Carolina Herpetological Society**
NC State Museum of Natural Sciences
11 West Jones St.
Raleigh, NC 27601-1029
www.ncherps.org

**Nebraska Herpetological Society**
c/o Department of Biology
University of Nebraska at Omaha
Omaha, NE 68182-0400
www.nebherp.org

**Southern Nevada Herpetological Society**
1955 North Decatur #106
Las Vegas, NV 89108-2209
(702) 646-6971
www.mcneely.net/sn_herp/

**New York Turtle and Tortoise Society**
P.O. Box 878
Orange, NJ 07051-0878
nytts.org

**Long Island Herpetological Society**
476 North Ontario Ave.
Lindenhurst, NY 11757
(631) 884-LIHS
www.lihs.org

**Northern Ohio Association of Herpetologists (NOAH)**
Dept. of Biology
Case Western Reserve University
Cleveland, OH 44106-7080
www.noahonline.net/mtlog/archives/
index.shtml

**Greater Cincinnati Herpetological Society**
P.O. Box 14783
Cincinnati, OH 45250
www.cincyherps.com

**Philadelphia Herpetological Society**
P.O. Box 52261
Philadelphia, PA 19115-7261
herpetology.com/phs.html

**Lehigh Valley Herpetological Society, Inc.**
609 North 4th St.
Allentown, PA 18102
members.tripod.com/~lvhs/

**Tennessee Herpetological Society**
3030 Wildlife Way
Morristown, TN 37814
home.mindspring.com/~froghaven/

**East Texas Herpetological Society**
P.O. Box 141
Katy, TX 77492-0141
www.eths.org

**Gulf Coast Turtle and Tortoise Society**
1227 Whitestone
Houston, TX 77073
(281) 443-3383
www.gctts.org

**West Texas Herpetological Society**
P.O. Box 60134
San Angelo, TX 76906
www.kingsnake.com/wths/

**South Texas Herpetology Association**
8023 Hill Trails
San Antonio, TX 78250-3008
www.kingsnake.com/stha/

**Virginia Herpetological Society**
Paul Sattler, VHS Secretary Treasurer
Dept. of Biology, Liberty University
1971 University Blvd.
Lynchburg, VA 24502
fwie.fw.vt.edu/VHS/

**Pacific Northwest Herpetological Society**
P.O. Box 547
Lakebay, WA 98349
www.pnhs.net

**Seattle Turtle & Tortoise Club**
23908 Bothell Everett Highway,
B-103
Bothell, WA 98021
(206) 291-7651
www.geocities.com/seattleturtleclub/

# Internet Resources

**Association of Reptilian and Amphibian Veterinarians (ARAV)**
*www.arav.org/Directory.htm*
This online ARAV membership directory lists members by state in the United States and by country or geographical region elsewhere.

**The Herp Vet Connection**
*www.herpvetconnection.com*
This site has a list of veterinarians recommended by reptile and amphibian owners worldwide, as well as links to veterinary sites and organizations.

**Kingsnake**
*www.kingsnake.com*
This granddaddy of reptiles and amphibians sites has links to care articles and suppliers, a photo gallery, message boards, classified ads, and news of herp shows and events.

**Melissa Kaplan's Chelonians**
*www.anapsid.org/mainchelonians.html*
Melissa Kaplan is well known as a reptile rescuer. You'll find articles here about just about every aspect of herp care, including finding a veterinarian, conservation, emergencies, and zoonoses.

**The Russian Tortoise**
*russiantortoise.org*
You'll find everything you ever wanted to know about the Russian Tortoise, including care sheets and a discussion forum.

**Sulcata Station**
*www.sulcata-station.org*
Complete information on Sulcata tortoises is on this site, including care sheets and FAQs.

**Tortoise Life**
*www.tortoiselife.co.uk*
This British site covers most tortoise species. You'll find care sheets and advice on husbandry and health care.

**Tortoise Trust**

*www.tortoisetrust.org*

Tortoise Trust is a nonprofit group dedicated to tortoise care and conservation. The site includes a discussion group, care sheets, and lots of other information.

**World Chelonian Trust**

*www.chelonia.org*

The World Chelonian Trust is dedicated to turtle conservation and education. The site includes articles, care sheets, and information on everything to do with turtles.

# Index

**Photo Credits**

*Michel Durand:* 36 (bottom)

*Lenny Flank:* 16, 24, 38 (top), 64, 69, 79, 93, 115

*Isabelle Francais:* 1, 11, 15, 19, 27, 28, 30 (top), 31 (bottom), 32 (bottom), 36 (top), 37 (bottom), 38 (bottom), 40–41, 42, 49, 50, 51, 53, 56, 58, 60, 61, 63, 65, 75, 78, 81, 91, 99, 100, 101, 110, 111

*Howell Book House:* 1

*Bill Love:* 4–5, 8–9, 12, 22, 23, 26, 29, 30 (bottom), 31 (top), 32 (top), 33, 34, 37 (top), 39, 43, 44, 54, 68, 72, 74, 82, 83, 84, 96–97, 103, 105, 106, 108, 112

*Tammy Rao:* 18, 46, 73, 87, 95, 98